CW00695053

Advanced Introduction to Private Law

Elgar Advanced Introductions are stimulating and thoughtful introductions to major fields in the social sciences and law, expertly written by the world's leading scholars. Designed to be accessible yet rigorous, they offer concise and lucid surveys of the substantive and policy issues associated with discrete subject areas.

The aims of the series are two-fold: to pinpoint essential principles of a particular field, and to offer insights that stimulate critical thinking. By distilling the vast and often technical corpus of information on the subject into a concise and meaningful form, the books serve as accessible introductions for undergraduate and graduate students coming to the subject for the first time. Importantly, they also develop well-informed, nuanced critiques of the field that will challenge and extend the understanding of advanced students, scholars and policy-makers.

For a full list of titles in the series please see the back of the book. Recent titles in the series include:

Advanced Introduction to

Private Law

JAN M. SMITS

Professor of European Private Law, Faculty of Law, Maastricht University, the Netherlands

Elgar Advanced Introductions

 Edward Elgar
PUBLISHING

Cheltenham, UK • Northampton, MA, USA

Published by
Edward Elgar Publishing Limited
The Lypiatts
15 Lansdown Road
Cheltenham
Glos GL50 2JA
UK

Edward Elgar Publishing, Inc.
William Pratt House
9 Dewey Court
Northampton
Massachusetts 01060
USA

A catalogue record for this book
is available from the British Library

Library of Congress Control Number: 2016944288

ISBN 978 1 78471 512 0 (cased)
ISBN 978 1 78471 514 4 (paperback)
ISBN 978 1 78471 513 7 (eBook)

Typeset by Servis Filmsetting Ltd, Stockport, Cheshire
Printed and bound in Great Britain by TJ International Ltd, Padstow

Contents

Preface

The aim of this small book is to make private law accessible and engaging to people who are not experts in the field. My goal is not to elucidate the many technical and detailed rules that private law consists of in each individual national jurisdiction, but rather to present the field as being about perennial normative questions on the legal aspect of relations among individuals. In doing so, private law is considered to be a unified field, of which the main branches – on contract, tort, property, family and succession – are governed by conflicts between private autonomy and countervailing principles.

Writing a non-parochial book such as this requires many choices that hopefully could be made without sacrificing accuracy. Unnecessary jargon is avoided and the law is placed as much as possible in the broader economic and social context. The main point this book tries to make is that, although similar societies may face similar problems, these problems can be solved in fundamentally different ways. What unites private lawyers is the *reasoning* that they deploy in facing these problems, not the uniformity of the outcomes they reach. It is this approach that allows me to 'disconnect' the many national variations of private law from what I see as the core questions in the field. Although most examples come from English, American, German and French law, the issues they illustrate apply to any jurisdiction. My mission is accomplished if the reader is convinced that private law is not about keeping lawyers or academics busy with entertaining puzzles, but is about designing rules that allow people to optimally flourish in daily life.

I wish to thank Eve Meurgey and Kate O'Reilly for invaluable help in preparing the manuscript and Ben Booth and his colleagues at Edward Elgar for their encouragement and guidance. I am also grateful to Bram Akkermans, Christa Dubois, Cees van Dam, Mark Kawakami, Daniel On, Hendrik Ploeger and Michael Wells-Greco for their willingness to comment on drafts.

Maastricht/Liège, 1 May 2016

1 Introduction: aims and contours of private law

1.1 Introduction

If someone were to ask what private law is about, a common answer would be that it deals with the rights and duties of individuals (including other private actors such as companies) with respect to one another. In this way, private law is usually contrasted with public law, which is about the organisation of the state and the relationship between the state and its citizens. We owe this grand division of the law into two main branches to the third-century Roman jurist Ulpian, who proclaimed private law to be about the well-being of individuals and public law to be about the common good.[1]

There is much to say about the accuracy of this distinction – which is at best a gradual one as no field of law can entirely neglect the public interest – but it still serves a useful purpose in structuring the law. At the core of private law lies the value that society wants to place upon people in pursuing their own individual goals without the need for authorisation by other people or the state.[2] Private law thus allows people to shape their own legal relations with others *by choice* and to enforce the ensuing rights in court whenever necessary. While the public interest is actively upheld by the state (which has received special powers to make this possible), private interests are only created and maintained if private individuals wish to do so. To give examples from all five major branches of private law: private law facilitates people in keeping or transferring their property; in making contracts about anything a person could wish (ranging from a simple purchase at the supermarket to employment and insurance) or to refrain from doing so; in claiming compensation for other peoples' unlawful conduct or to turn the other cheek on the wrongdoer; in deciding to marry, to divorce and whether to have children; and, finally, in disposing of one's

---

1 Digest 1, 1, 1, 2.
2 Lucy 2009, 58–9.

property after death or relying on the default rules of succession. In this sense, private law forms the backbone of civil society. It allows people to flourish in matters of economy, work, leisure and family (in the words of Aristotle: to live 'the good life') or to take the deliberate decision *not* to do so.[3]

Although, with this, the starting point of private law lies in the exercise of autonomy by individuals it is far from it that autonomy always prevails. In reality, it competes with a wide range of countervailing considerations that are informed by other public concerns than just allowing autonomy. For example, the norms of equality and non-discrimination, though developed for the relationship between the state and its citizens, also express essential values throughout all fields of private law. Equally, the autonomy of the owner in property law is limited by the interests of third parties and by the underlying rationale of the proper distribution of scarce resources in society. In the same vein, many jurisdictions' law of succession restricts the freedom of testation in order to protect the deceased's family members. Private law has several hearts beating simultaneously.

This book approaches private law from this interaction between autonomy and other societal interests in an effort to do away with its extreme specialisation, which is rightly considered to be one of the main problems of present-day legal scholarship. The different branches of law are often treated as isolated compartments, an approach that has long been standard in the common law world where, for example, contracts, torts and property are still today seen as separate subjects. This was once different in the continental civil law tradition, where private law was considered as one comprehensive field governed by unifying principles. This has changed in the course of the twentieth century with the unfortunate result that intersections, inconsistencies and gaps between sub-fields are no longer explored, although it is through this that a creative development of the law is made possible.

Given that private law deals with the crucial task of ordering private relationships, it is no surprise that the field never suffered from a lack of academic interest. Ever since the birth of the University in eleventh-century Europe, it has been part of the core curriculum. In continental Europe it was taught in the form of Roman law, which subsequently came to serve as the basis for the learned *ius commune* that united

---

3 Aristotle, *Nicomachean Ethics*; Dagan 2015, 10.

much of continental Europe and was applicable in practice unless local statutes or customs ruled differently on a certain point.[4] The main reason for this remarkable 'second life' of Roman law – originating from essentially the years 0–250 – was that its contents, and in particular the sixth-century compilation of it by Emperor Justinian now known as the *Corpus Iuris Civilis*, were seen as the most authoritative source on how to conduct oneself in private relationships. The study of private law thus took place in Latin by an international audience of students who – because of the unity of the material – could pick and choose the law faculty of their liking anywhere in Europe. It was only with the enactment of civil law codifications in the nineteenth century – which took until 1900 in Germany – that this modern use of Roman law (the *usus modernus*) was replaced with as many national laws as there were countries. In England, however, the situation was slightly different: although English universities did not regard the common law as worthy of study until William Blackstone became the first professor of English law at the University of Oxford in 1758, 'civil law' (i.e. Roman law) was taught at both the universities of Oxford and Cambridge since their founding.

These ancient origins of private law should not conceal its current vitality. As any other part of the law, it stands in close relationship to economic developments and to changing views in society of what is 'the right thing to do'. Scholars and practitioners around the world have taken up this challenge. To give examples from each of the fields discussed in this book: how to ensure effective enforcement of contracts? Can tort play a role in reducing carbon emissions? Should credits earned in online-games be regarded as property? Ought cohabiting partners who split up be treated in the same way as divorcees? Are relatives to inherit or is the estate of the deceased to be used for the common good? These, and other, questions show the richness of private law and its relevance to people's day-to-day life.

Two issues require a separate treatment in this introduction: the actors involved in the making of private law (Section 1.2) and the aims, if any, that private law seeks to achieve (Section 1.3). The order of the book is sketched in Section 1.4.

---

4 Zimmermann 1990.

1.2   Actors in the making of private law

Law is always made through an intricate interplay of different legal actors. A layperson may believe that the will of the legislator is both necessary and sufficient to change existing laws, but in reality the authority of the law is established in a much more complicated process, in which courts, academics and those affected by the law ('private actors') also play their part. These actors need not only exist at the national level. In particular, in Europe private law is now also very much a multilevel system with rules not only emanating from the national institutions but also from the European Union legislator and court in Luxembourg and from the European Convention on Human Rights (ECHR) and the court in Strasbourg. In addition, there are a number of worldwide conventions of which the Convention on Contracts for the International Sale of Goods 1980 is no doubt the biggest success story. However, this should not conceal the different emphasis that jurisdictions put on the importance of legislation and case law. Here the big divide is between civil law and common law countries.

In the civil law family, predominant in continental Europe, Africa and South America, legislation in the form of a civil code is the principal source of private law. Chief examples of such codes are the French *Code Civil* of 1804 and the German *Bürgerliches Gesetzbuch* (BGB) of 1900. Both codes were introduced after revolutionary events, namely the French Revolution of 1789 and the German unification in 1871. In both cases, the code put an end to the legal diversity that previously existed in both France and the 39 independent German states. This reveals two important aspects of codification: it is not only a way to unify previously diverse laws, but is also the instrument through which a national legislator is able to restate, simplify, consolidate and change the existing law, and thus make a new start. Codification abolishes the old law. The illustrative anecdote is of the French law professor, Bugnet, who, in the early nineteenth century, told his students: 'I know nothing of civil law; I only teach the Code Napoleon'.

While codification thus prioritises the (democratic) legislator, this does not makes case law obsolete. This was indeed the naïve view of the first codifiers who tried to cover every possible situation, the Prussian Civil Code of 1794 (the *Allgemeines Landrecht*) being a frightening example with its no less than 19,000 articles. We still find a reminiscence of this fear of too powerful courts in Art. 5 of the French Civil Code, stating that '[t]he courts shall be prohibited from issuing rules which take the form of general and binding decisions on those cases which are submitted to them'. Reality is different. The Code is sometimes not only silent but also needs interpretation in the light of the circumstances of the case and changed views in society of what is right. The older the civil code, the more important it therefore is to take note of the decisions of the highest national court in civil law matters, such as the German *Bundesgerichtshof* and the French *Cour de Cassation*. Art. 1 of the Swiss Civil Code (1907) is a good reflection of how important the task of the court can still be as it assigns the court with the task of acting as a substitute legislator: '[i]f the Code does not furnish an applicable provision, the judge shall decide in accordance with customary law, and failing that, according to the rule which he would establish as legislator'.

In the universe of the common lawyer, it is not primarily the task of the legislator to develop the law. The dominant source of private law in England and in almost the entire English-speaking world beyond Britain, including the United States, Australia and India, is not legislation but the case law of the courts. This does not mean that specific statutes on private law are absent. They just do not aim to systematise comprehensively the existing law, nor do they make it redundant to consult judicial decisions. The main explanation for this emphasis on case law lies in history:[5] while civil law on the European continent was unified by way of national codification in the newly created nation-states of the nineteenth century, the highly fragmented local statutes and customs William the Conqueror found in England after the Norman Conquest of 1066 had by that time already been unified by the King's court. This centralisation and unification was completed as early as around 1500, and from that time onwards it was possible to speak literally of one 'common law'. Nineteenth-century attempts in Britain to replace this judge-made law by a codification understandably failed: codification was not needed as a weapon against legal diversity and neither was it necessary to use it to build a nation. In addition, the ruling class regarded the idea of codification as too revolutionary. As a result, English common law could develop uninterrupted: old case law was never 'abolished', leading to some 350,000 published cases all being in principle still relevant today.

As regards legal academics, their role is no longer very different in civil and common law. In both legal traditions, their main activity is to

---

5 Van Caenegem 1992.

comment on legal developments and to systematise the law by developing principles and concepts with a view to their application in future cases. This should not conceal that the interaction between academia and the official lawmaking institutions does differ within national legal communities. Academic criticism can turn a legislative provision into a dead letter in some civil law jurisdictions, including Germany.[6] It would also be impossible to understand the genesis of the German Civil Code without considering the *Pandektenwissenschaft* of the nineteenth century preceding it. The Code, seen by many as the highpoint of intellectual learning of that time, consists of a sophisticated structure closely following the Pandectist system[7] with a general part and separate books devoted to, respectively, the Law of Obligations, Property Law, Family Law and Succession Law. The influence of this system can still be detected in civil codes around the world, including those of the Netherlands, Japan and Korea. Still today, academic writing has great persuasive authority in Germany and is often quoted by the courts. This stands in contrast to England, where, at least until recently, only deceased authors could be cited under the rule 'Better read when dead'.

An increasingly important role in the shaping of private law is played by rules drafted by others than the official actors. This soft law can take the form of, for example, restatements, guidelines, principles and model rules. Although soft law by its definition is not binding 'hard' law, it is still important in practice. Not only are these rules often a first step towards adopting a binding instrument (legislators tend to look at soft law as a blueprint for future legislation) but they also reflect the more progressive *opinio juris*, which is the direction in which the law is to develop according to the cutting-edge opinion makers. This aspirational aspect of soft law can make it a useful source in interpreting and criticising existing laws as well as in teaching the law. Examples are the widely used *Restatements of the Law* published by the American Law Institute on topics such as property, torts, contracts, succession and trusts. They have a worldwide counterpart in the Unidroit Principles of International Commercial Contracts (PICC) and European equivalents in the Principles of European Contract Law (PECL), European Tort Law (PETL) and European Family Law (PEFL) and the Draft Common Frame of Reference of European Private Law (DCFR) that all aim to identify commonalities among jurisdictions.

---

6 Jansen 2010.
7 Heise 1807.

Implicit in the above overview of legal actors is that private law is largely organised along national lines. Legislators, courts and academics function primarily within their own national communities and speak to each other in their own local language. This is in line with the heritage of Montesquieu that each nation chooses a law specific to that nation's 'spirit' in order to help define its national identity.[8] It poses a difficulty in writing about private law as a universal subject. This book adopts the view that the similar conflict between autonomy and countervailing principles discussed in Section 1.1 underlies not only all fields of private law but can also be found in any random jurisdiction. This clears the way for discussing the law in much the same way as an economist discusses economic questions, or a biologist looks at nature: in a non-parochial way and therefore not restricted to the law of one particular country.

1.3   The aims of private law

To many working in the field of private law it is unnecessary to ask which aims private law seeks to achieve. They reason that if this field regulates the legal relationships among individuals there is no need to bother about any deeper goals, if existent at all. When working in practice, they just apply the rules of legislators and highest courts to reach decisions in concrete cases. When academics, they further develop the so-called doctrinal system of private law. However, this 'just do it' mentality neglects what economist John Maynard Keynes once wrote, namely that 'practical men who believe themselves to be quite exempt from any intellectual influence are usually the slaves . . . of some academic scribbler of a few years back'.[9] Any practice is based on underlying theoretical presumptions. Although this book is not about big and deep theories, Keynes' wisecrack does prompt the need for a further, brief investigation of the nature of private law. Two schools of thought make competing claims.

The first school asserts that private law works primarily as an instrument to reach some external goal. This goal is often found in economic efficiency.[10] This implies, for example, that contracts must only be enforced if they promote social welfare by making both parties to

---

8 Montesquieu 1748.
9 Keynes 1936, 383.
10 Posner 2014.

the contract better off. Similarly, an economic justification of tort law would emphasise that the sum of the costs of accidents and the costs of avoiding these accidents have to be minimised in order to obtain optimal deterrence of future wrongful behaviour. Another variation of private law as a means to an end is to make the success (hence the adoption) of a rule dependent on whether this rule influences behaviour of individuals in the way desired. In this view, the only reason why private law influences people is because it creates incentives for the right behaviour or penalises wrong behaviour. For example, one could argue that the reason why the property of debtors unwilling to pay their debt can be seized is because this creates an incentive for debtors properly to perform their contracts.[11] Empirical legal studies are mostly based upon this utilitarian idea that the law functions because it attaches consequences to behaviour. Still a third variation of private law as a means to an end is to consider it from the perspective of distributive justice. Building upon Aristotle's distinction between corrective and distributive justice[12] it is then argued that private law, like tax law or constitutional law, must deal with the latter, i.e. the fair (re)allocation of resources such as wealth, income and liberties among the members of the political community. This type of justice would then also apply to contract[13] and tort law, refuting the standard view that these areas are about corrective (or commutative) justice in that they deal with interpersonal rights and wrongs or, in more difficult language, with correcting any interference of fair distribution in a specific relationship between two people.

Much can be said against these external views in which private law is only an instrument to reach some outside goal. Thus, economic analysis has long since been criticised for its lack of arguments as to why efficiency is the desirable goal of the law.[14] Equally problematic is the presumption of empiricists that people only act under the influence of incentives or sanctions. There is no empirical basis for this: people may well follow rules simply because they want to obey the law without thinking about extra-legal sanctions at all.[15] Accepting the third variation of private law as aiming for distributive justice would imply that all interactions between individuals must be evaluated in view of this

---

11 Smith 2011, 218.
12 Aristotle, *Nicomachean Ethics*, Book V, 2–5.
13 Kronman 1980.
14 A much criticised counterattack was launched by Kaplow and Shavell 2002.
15 Smith 2011, 216.

criterion. But if private law is there to pursue the common good of 'social' justice, it is in fact public law. This view of all law being public law has a long ancestry, from the great American jurist Oliver Wendell Holmes, who described all law as being about undifferentiated interaction between government and citizen, to the Critical Legal Studies-movement of the 1970s. However, this denies that the relationship among individuals is governed by other legal values than the relationship between state and citizens. There are things the state should not be involved in. To borrow an example from Lucy: the decision to buy my coffee from Costa and not from Small Café could affect the makeup of my local high street but we believe my decision to buy coffee at one place instead of at another is not a public issue.[16]

This does not mean that elements of distributive justice cannot play a role in private relationships[17] but it goes too far to assess all of private law from the perspective of the fair distribution of resources. In reality, there are elements of both the private and the public in any field of the law. For example, tort law belongs to private law in that one individual (the victim) can decide whether he wants to exercise his power to hold the defendant liable and claim compensation. But it is also a public value that people can hold other persons responsible for the wrongs they commit. In the same vein, the division of property over members of society is a question of distributive justice but this does not mean the government must intervene for the sake of a fair *re*-distribution every time a seller decides to transfer an object to somebody else. So nothing prevents us from saying that in each field we have rules aiming to allocate collective goods *and* aiming to redress what went wrong in an individual transaction.

The second school of thought regards private law not as pursuing some outside goal, but as a normative system that intends to guide people's behaviour.[18] This is also the view adopted in this book: private law provides legal rules on how individuals must conduct themselves vis-à-vis others. Private law excels in – to give only three examples – articulating when a contract must be performed, when money needs to be paid for wrongful conduct or when people are allowed to marry. This view has two important advantages compared to the instrumental one. First, the focus on the question of how people should legally treat each

---

16 Lucy 2009, 48; Bydlinski 1996, 684.
17 As Weinrib 1995 argues.
18 Smith 2011.

other opens the door to involving social norms, i.e. norms specifying what is acceptable in a society or group. These norms – such as good faith in contract law, business custom in commercial law and the ordinarily prudent person in tort law – are important but sit uneasily in an instrumental view. It is through these social norms that the law can reflect changing societal views of what is right. This pays heed to the insight that people owe each other duties without the state telling them this is the case – contrary to a long tradition in which the law is presented as commands issued by the sovereign power with the ultimate authority grounded in whatever is seen as the basis for the authority of the sovereign (God, 'We the People' or Parliament).

A second advantage of a view of private law as articulating norms of conduct is that it gives pride of place to legal doctrine. An instrumental view of the law has difficulty in understanding the proper role of the doctrinal system because it does not seem to reflect non-legal objectives. However, reality shows it is the legal system judges turn to when they need to decide a case, and practitioners use the legal system when advising their clients. This makes perfect sense in a normative view of law: legal doctrine represents the highly subtle normative complexity of the law and is thus a source of information on how to behave.

1.4   Order of this book

It was just argued that private law enables people to flourish in matters of economy, work, leisure and family by allowing them to shape their legal relations with others by choice. The fact that a person has the freedom to contract, to hold another liable in tort, to have property, to found a family and to dispose of his inheritance after death are central to this aim. It is therefore no surprise that the five institutions of contract, tort, property, family and succession form the basis for the traditional ordering of private law. This book also adheres to this structure. It starts off with two chapters on the law of obligations (contract and tort) and continues with discussing property law, family law and the law of succession. The epilogue provides a brief conclusion.

2 Contract law

2.1 Introduction

We live in a contract society.[1] Individuals rely to a large extent on the agreements they voluntarily enter into to obtain the products and services they require. Unlike the situation in pre-modern societies, when people were dependent on their own family and household to be fed, clothed and cared for, we trust people to shape their legal relations with others by choice.[2] This puts contracts at the very core of private law. The state guarantees a sphere of individual self-determination by allowing people to conclude the contracts they like and thus to pursue the goals they find valuable in life. It makes contract law not only the main tool to facilitate and regulate economic transactions and to allow for division of labour,[3] but also a means for individuals to pursue their own perception of the good. At the same time, however, it is exactly this emphasis on private autonomy that becomes the Achilles' heel of many contracts. As long as an agreement is the result of free bargaining among socially and economically equal parties, each party is likely to benefit from the contract. But reality may be different: consumer-buyers, insurees, tenants, employees and smaller businesses often simply have to accept the terms dictated to them by their economically stronger and more experienced counterparts. This explains why the two simultaneously beating hearts of contract law are the one that allows allocating resources through exchange and the one that is concerned with realising a minimum amount of fairness among the contracting parties to avoid abuse of bargaining power.

A great variety of contract types exist. Although laypeople often associate contracts only with a piece of paper through which they buy a

---

1 Weber 1922, 399.
2 The cliché reference is to Maine 1861, 170: the movement of societies 'has hitherto been a movement from Status to Contract'.
3 Smith 1776, Book I, ch. 2, 3.

house or take up a job the law uses a much broader definition. In any given jurisdiction contracts are defined as legally binding agreements, irrespective of whether they are written down or not. This means that, in law, people conclude binding contracts when they buy products in a supermarket, take out insurance, download software, see their doctor, go to the hairdresser or open up a franchise. Contracts can also come about in cases where no words have been exchanged, as in the case of putting money into a coffee machine or computerised derivatives trading. In recent decades the importance of contracting has increased even more as a result of the privatisation of public services: water, electricity, telecom and waste management that used to be provided for by the state are now often being contracted out to 'the market'. Contract is even used as an instrument to reduce global warming by allowing polluters to buy and sell greenhouse gas emission rights. If polluters want to increase their emissions, they need to buy permits from other polluters willing to sell theirs, presumably leading to pollution at the lowest possible cost to society.[4]

This chapter presents the main questions contract law seeks to answer. Lawyers tend to structure these questions in accordance with the life-cycle of the contract: when is a binding contract formed, what does the contract oblige the parties to do and what remedies are available if the other party does not act in accordance with these obligations? These three questions on, respectively, formation, contents and contractual remedies are discussed in Sections 2.3, 2.4 and 2.5. They are preceded by Section 2.2, which is devoted to the principles underlying the law of contract and the role of the lawmaker in regulating private transactions.

2.2   Principles of contract law

Modern contract law is to a large extent a by-product of the rise of capitalism. Although the possibility to conclude binding contracts had been instrumental to international merchants for a long time before, it was only with the Industrial Revolution of the eighteenth and nineteenth centuries that the golden age of contracts came about. Horwitz speaks of the 'triumph of contract'.[5] While in a previous era contracts

---

4 See, e.g., EU-Directive 2003/87 establishing a scheme for greenhouse gas emission allowance trading and the 'cap-and-trade' system in place in California since 2012.
5 Horwitz 1977, 160.

were only enforced if the exchange was regarded as just and fair and not used to exploit the other party, the principles guiding the law from then onwards were those of contractual freedom and binding force purely based on the parties' consent. These two principles of contractual freedom and binding force are still the guiding principles of contract law today.

The principle of freedom of contract makes contract law special compared to other areas of the law. The question of what is the law (in the sense of the enforceable rights and obligations of the parties) can generally be decided upon by the parties themselves. Contractual freedom entails that parties are not only free to decide whether they want to contract at all, and with whom, but also what the contents of their contract will be.[6] No one is obliged to enter into a contract, but if one does, one is bound by it in the same way as if the rules had been made by the democratically elected legislator. The French Civil Code of 1804 – drafted in the heyday of the autonomy of the individual citizen – succinctly encapsulates this principle of binding force in its famous Art. 1103: '[a]greements lawfully entered into have force of law for those who have made them'.[7] Unlike tort, already identified by Gaius in the year 160 as the other main source of obligations,[8] a contract creates a bond between a creditor and debtor because they *want* to be bound, not because the law obliges them to.

If contracts freely entered into are indeed binding upon the parties, as the law suggests, there is no need for a separate test of fairness. Individuals are in a better position than anyone else – including a judge – to decide what is in their best interest. If they then conclude a contract conscious of its consequences, it is fair to hold these individuals to what they agreed upon. The famous French aphorism is: '*Qui dit contractuel dit juste*' ('the contractual is fair in and of itself'). The British judge George Jessel concurred: 'if there is one thing more than another which public policy requires, it is that men of full age and competent understanding shall have the utmost liberty of contracting and that their contracts, when entered into freely and voluntarily, shall be held sacred and shall be enforced by Courts of Justice'.[9]

---

6 Cf. Arts. 1:102 PECL and 1.1 PICC.

7 Art. 1134 until the reform through Ordonnance 2016-131.

8 Gaius, Institutes III, 88: '*Omnis enim obligatio vel ex contractu nascitur, vel ex delicto*'.

9 *Printing and Numerical Registering Co v Sampson* (1875) 19 Eq 462 (CoA).

This view still largely forms the basis for our present-day contract law, be it that even the most liberal of contract lawyers accept that the conditions under which contractual autonomy is exercised are often flawed, and that the law therefore needs to intervene at times to protect one party against the other. Not everybody has the same degree of free will to promise what they want. A party could mislead its counterpart by lying about the qualities of the sold product, preventing the latter to form his intention in the right way (which would often allow the deceived party to invalidate the contract for reason of misrepresentation or fraud). It could also be that a party is presumed to lack the necessary judgement because of age or mental illness (which would be a case of legal incapacity). In consumer contracts, the law often requires the professional party to give all kinds of information to the consumer so that the latter can take an informed decision before entering into the contract. The court also has the power to strike down manifestly unfair terms used in general conditions. These are all devices aiming to redress the unequal position among the parties.[10] In addition, legislators have come up with a myriad of mandatory laws in contracts such as employment, residential lease, consumer credit and consumer sale. In these contracts so little is left of the parties' freedom to set the terms of their agreement that they are often referred to as 'regulated contracts'.

An important question is whether contract law should only aim to redress an imbalance in parties' bargaining position or should also be used as an instrument to (re)distribute wealth. This would push contract law back to its pre-nineteenth century position as a means to realise substantive justice.[11] Today's society, however, regards the redressing of differences in income and wealth as the mission of politics, which does so by way of progressive taxation. A court would become a highly political institution if it were to assess whether each specific contract contributes to social justice or not. More importantly, no 'stronger' contracting party would still be willing to conclude a contract with a 'weaker' one if a court would be able to strike it down for reason of unfairness – let alone the difficulty of attempting to reach a consensus on what a 'fair' outcome would be in a contractual context.[12] Instead, contract law is built upon the highly democratic assumption that today's buyer is tomorrow's seller and that therefore both should

---

10 Some of these techniques are discussed in Sections 2.3 and 2.4.
11 Cf. Gordley 2006, 292.
12 Kronman 1980.

be treated equally. This is reflected in the wish to provide rules as 'practical tools for practical men', as the American scholar Karl Llewellyn once remarked.[13]

This down-to-earth stance stands in stark contrast to the sophisticated academic discussion about why it is that contracts bind. Theories abound. The traditional explanation is that a contract must be enforced because the parties freely intended to be legally bound,[14] or at least were able to reasonably rely on the other party's intention. These agreement or reliance theories focusing on the (apparent) meeting of minds are rejected by those who find the reason for a contract's binding nature in the party's promise: '[s]ince a contract is first of all a promise, the contract must be kept because a promise must be kept'.[15] To Fried this is purely a matter of respect for individual autonomy and trust. A third view seeks the reason why contracts should be enforced in the idea that free exchange between individuals maximises value. This instrumental view emphasises that a voluntary exchange satisfies the preferences of both parties: each of them gives up something valuable in return for something they regard as even more valuable.[16] On this view, Adam Smith's invisible hand is not far away: if each contracting party pursues his own self-interest, society as a whole will also be better off. Still a fourth theory, based on the Aristotelian idea of virtue, regards contracts as binding in so far as they promote human flourishing and virtuous moral behaviour. Practically speaking, this means that exploitative or grossly unfair contracts are not enforceable.[17] Each of these theories has been severely criticised and it is likely they all contain some valuable element that helps to explain why contracts are enforceable.

If contract law is unique among the legal disciplines in the freedom it leaves parties to devise their own rules, what role does this leave for the lawmaker? It was already mentioned that legislators and courts will still have to set the boundaries for freedom of contract in order to ensure equal bargaining power. In addition, they have to guard against contracts being contrary to mandatory laws, public order or good morals. For example, the law must invalidate the sale of nuclear arms

---

13 Llewellyn 1939, 779.
14 See, e.g., Von Savigny 1840–49, Vol. 3, 258.
15 Fried 1981, 17; see also Flume 1992, 5.
16 Posner 2014, 10–11.
17 Markovits 2014.

to a terrorist group or the 'voluntary' waiver of fundamental rights, such as the promise of the purchaser of a house no longer to exercise his religion in return for a lower price on the contract.

The most important role of the lawmaker, however, is to provide for so-called 'default rules'. Contracting parties often only agree on a few main points ('8 chairs as seen by the buyer, €300 each, payment upon delivery on 20 May') and do not bother about anything else (such as the place of delivery and the rights of buyer and seller in case of non-performance). This is perfectly sensible behaviour. First, because the great majority of parties cannot conceive of all possible contingencies that could happen during the course of the contract. This is particularly true if the contract is intended to last for a long period of time, as in the case of a residential lease or distribution contract. Second, because in most cases it is not efficient to negotiate and draft contracts that foresee all possible contingencies. The contract would have to represent a high value to invest the time and money to make this worthwhile. The law therefore relieves parties of the burden of drafting and negotiating their own rules by providing defaults that are automatically applicable if the parties have not made any other arrangements. It is thus extremely useful for parties to be able to rely on default provisions like those requiring the quality of goods sold to be satisfactory[18] or stipulating the payment of rent is due at the beginning of the lease period.[19] Each system of national contract law typically has hundreds of such background provisions.

The question that has bewildered legislators in recent decades is whether the provision of default (or even mandatory) rules for contracts should still take place at the national level. Globalisation of markets suggests that contract laws must become more international. This would have the inestimable benefit of companies and consumers no longer needing to delve into the intricacies of a foreign law to find out about their exact rights and obligations. However, there is always a trade-off between centrally imposed legal uniformity and the wish of a jurisdiction to cater to the preferences of its own constituency. Even in the United States there is no federal act on sales law, let alone on uniform contract law in general because the US Congress has no wish to interfere with the states' powers in this field. Instead it leaves each of the 50 individual states free to adopt a model law in the form of the

---

18 S. 9(1) UK Consumer Rights Act 2015.
19 § 556b (1) BGB.

Uniform Commercial Code (UCC). Article 2 UCC on sales has been highly successful, with all the states, with the exception of Louisiana, having adopted it.

The European Union legislator follows a different path and requires member states to implement so-called 'directives' into each national legal order. Most of these directives deal with some aspect of consumer contracts, such as unfair clauses in general conditions, remedies in case of non-conformity and the right to withdraw from contracts concluded over the Internet.[20] Yet another solution is proffered to commercial parties who contract across borders. In case they are located in one of the 84 states that has ratified the Convention on Contracts for the International Sale of Goods 1980 (CISG), their contract is automatically subject to the default rules of that convention on formation and remedies. This, as such, does not guarantee uniformity: in the absence of an international court the application of the CISG lies in the hands of national lawyers and judges. They are likely to be subject to a homeward trend, the tendency to interpret the CISG in line with the domestic law.[21] The ensuing diversity in interpretation is one of the reasons why parties regularly exclude the CISG and prefer a more certain choice for the law of one national jurisdiction.

2.3   Formation of contract

As long as economic activity only consists of exchanging goods on the spot (as was presumably the case in early societies), there is no urgent need to answer the question of when a binding contract is formed. This is different from the moment a party promises to do or to give something in the future. The law must then decide whether this promise is enforceable, meaning the promisee can go to court and force the promisor to, for example, deliver the good or pay the price. The law certainly does not always provide this badge of enforceability. If I promise my fiancée to take her to dinner tomorrow evening, no sensible person would claim that she can legally force me to feed her. Of the vast majority of promises we make in our life, it is at best morally wrong not to keep them. Breaking a promise may also have many negative consequences for the

---

20 Respectively, EU-Directives 93/13 on unfair terms in consumer contracts, 1999/44 on sale of consumer goods and 2011/83 on consumer rights.

21 As in *Raw Materials Inc v Manfred Forberich GmbH* 2004 WL 1535839 (N.D. Ill. 2004), in which a US District Court applied the UCC in interpreting Art. 79 CISG on *force majeure*.

friends we keep, the people we love and the reputation we have – but none of this is the law's business. A contrary view would make society unliveable and would flood the courts with futile cases.

All modern jurisdictions seek the test for the enforceability of a promise in the intention of the parties to be legally bound. Article 2:101 of the PECL succinctly states the accepted view everywhere regarding this issue: a contract is concluded 'if the parties intend to be legally bound' and 'reach a sufficient agreement'.[22] Both elements deserve attention.

The question whether there is an intention to be legally bound is not a matter of psychology, but a legal question: the law decides when such an intention exists. It is usually not a problem to 'find' the intention in cases where the respective promises of the parties are more or less of the same value, or if the parties are sophisticated business people who can take care of their own interests. However, the law is much more reluctant to enforce purely gratuitous promises or promises among family members or friends. It is simply less likely that someone would wish to be legally bound in these situations. A purely gratuitous promise, such as the promise to make a gift, is even viewed with so much suspicion most civil law jurisdictions require this promise to be put in a notarial deed.[23] This forces the donor to think through his act of benevolence and allows an independent notary (in most countries a trained lawyer) to warn the donor of the consequences of his act. Under common law, a gratuitous promise is equally unenforceable, but for the reason that it lacks consideration. Consideration demands a *quid pro quo*: the promise must be given for a (promise of) counter-performance by the other party and a gratuitous promise clearly lacks this. In the absence of a notary, the common law requires the donative promise to be put in a deed. This written and signed document attested by witnesses may not offer the same security as a notarial deed common in the civil law jurisdictions, but it does make the donor reflect upon his plan to perform an act of altruism and forces him to put his promise in precise writing.[24]

The second element required for a binding contract is sufficient agreement among the parties. The question whether this agreement exists

22 Art. 2:101 Principles of European Contract Law, see www.jus.uio.no/lm/eu.contract.principles.parts.1.to.3.2002.
23 See, e.g., Art. 931 French *Code Civil* and § 518 BGB.
24 Smits 2014, 101.

is usually answered by dissecting the contracting process into an offer and an acceptance. Agreement (sometimes referred to with the Latin phrase *consensus ad idem*) only exists if one party (the offeror) made a valid offer and the other party (the offeree) accepted it. The offer and acceptance model was developed in the seventeenth and eighteenth centuries when trade and travel expanded and contracts were increasingly concluded among people who could not see each other face to face. Each jurisdiction has highly detailed rules allowing it to identify an offer, whether it can be revoked and what is the exact moment in time when the contract comes into being upon acceptance. These rules have great practical importance. If the display of goods in a shop or an advertisement on a news-site qualifies as an offer – which French law states that it does – the seller cannot go back on his intention. This is clearly in the interest of the prospective buyer, who may have been tempted to enter the seller's shop or respond to the advertisement because of the attractiveness of the product on offer. English and American law adopt the opposite position and reserve the seller the right not to enter into a contract with the interested person.[25] This purportedly puts the seller in a better position to negotiate, although it is difficult to see the value of this argument in a world dominated by Carrefour, Wal-Mart and H&M, where haggling and negotiating for the price is generally not something the customer is supposed to do.

The law's position that a party is only bound to a contract if it has expressed its (apparent) intention to enter into a legal relationship assumes people have control over what they intend and are able to assess what is in their best interest. This, however, is not always the case. The law adopts a variety of techniques to ensure people are only bound in cases where their intention is freely given and sufficiently informed. It was already mentioned that a party must not lie about the qualities of the product at the risk of rescission for reason of misrepresentation or fraud. It was also noted earlier that the law presumes that minors and mentally disabled persons lack the necessary understanding, judgement and experience to bind themselves. Formalities also fit this picture. Although a simple agreement between the parties usually suffices, some contracts have to be put in writing (typically consumer credit and timeshare[26]) or even made up in the form of a (notarial) deed. This prevents parties, at least in theory, from carelessly binding

---

25 *Fisher v Bell* [1961] 1 QB 394 (HC); Burrows 2016, s. 7(5).
26 See, e.g., EU-Directive 2008/48 on credit agreements for consumers and EU-Directive 2008/122 on timeshare.

themselves without much aforethought. Yet another device to make a party's consent freer and better informed is to allow withdrawal from the contract within a short period of time after the conclusion of the contract or the delivery of the goods.[27] During this 'cooling-off period' the buyer can reconsider his consent in case aggressive sales techniques were used (as in doorstep selling or telemarketing) or where the buyer was unable to form an accurate picture of the product (as in the case of contracts concluded over the Internet). Seeing a photo of a product on a website is different from being able actually to touch and feel that same product.

However, the most used regulatory technique to ensure informed consent is mandatory disclosure of information. Legislators around the world require professional parties to inform consumers about a wide range of topics concerning the product or service they offer. In the European Union such pre-contractual information duties exist for timeshare, package travel, doorstep sale, distance selling and consumer credit. In the United States, state laws mandate disclosure for an ever-greater variety of contracts, even to such an extent that the term 'disclosure empire' was coined.[28] The rule that the consumer must have had the opportunity to read the general conditions before being bound also fits this tendency, as do health warnings on food, alcohol and cigarettes. The legislator's motive for mandatory disclosure is to remedy the consumer's informational disadvantage and thus to restore his autonomy in contracting. However, serious doubts exist as to whether more information in fact leads to better decisions. Ben-Shahar and Schneider make the convincing argument that consumers usually do not read disclosed information. In one experiment a software developer put a clause in a license agreement promising $1,000 to the first user to respond. It took four months and 3,000 downloads before anyone replied. Even more concerning is that if people bother to read the information, they may not understand the content, or if they do understand it they are incapable of using the information to make better purchasing decisions.[29] This makes mandatory disclosure perhaps not harmful, but also not particularly useful in empowering consumers.

---

27 Fourteen days in the case of doorstep selling, distance contracts, timeshare and consumer credit in the EU; three days for doorstep sales under US federal law, but more generous periods in state laws.

28 Ben-Shahar and Schneider 2014, 26. The federal Truth in Lending Act 1968 also requires disclosure of interest rates and credit terms.

29 Ben-Shahar and Schneider 2014, 42 ff; 2011, 671.

2.4   The contents of the contract

The question of what the parties must do and not do under a contract may seem redundant to some. If the parties' rights and obligations follow from the party agreement and, if needed, from the default rules that come to supplement it, how could there be uncertainty about the contents of the contract? In legal practice, however, this is the most common source of contract disputes. Three issues in particular can lead to controversy: what circumstances give rise to a duty of disclosure of certain facts, how should the party agreement be interpreted and can 'unfair' contract terms be set aside?

The answer to all three questions is dependent on the extent to which the law is willing to help a party who did not exercise all due care itself. Not all jurisdictions adopt the same view on this. Civil law jurisdictions tend to emphasise that contracting parties have to take into account each other's interests because they form, as it was once put by the French author René Demogue, a 'microcosm' in which both parties work towards a common goal. This means that courts are willing to help parties, enabled by the provision typical for civil codes that parties are to act in accordance with good faith ('reasonableness and fairness'). This principle can also be found in the American Restatement.[30] In a more liberal – and perhaps commercially more viable – legal system, parties are allowed to contract at arm's length, which is the position of English law. For example, in a case about contract negotiations the House of Lords held that 'the concept of a duty to carry on negotiations in good faith is inherently repugnant to the adversarial position of the parties when involved in negotiations. Each party to the negotiations is entitled to pursue his (or her) own interest . . .'[31] This fits the emphasis English law puts on the predictability of the outcome of a case. Roy Goode wrote, not without reason, that 'it is necessary in a commercial setting that businessmen at least should know where they stand . . . The last thing that we want to do is to drive business away by vague concepts of fairness which make judicial decisions unpredictable'.[32]

These different mentalities clearly affect the question of when a party must disclose certain facts to its counterpart. Should the vendor of a house mention that the floors underneath the carpet are rotten,

---

30 Restatement (Second) of Contracts § 205 (1981).
31 *Walford v Miles* [1992] 2 AC 128 (HL) *per* Lord Ackner.
32 Goode 1992.

or should the purchaser be required to investigate this for himself? English law traditionally adopts the maxim of *caveat emptor* or 'let the buyer beware'. This is a clear incentive for a party to be careful and take initiative in informing itself before concluding the contract. Civil law jurisdictions are more often willing to assume that a party must inform its counterpart about the qualities or saleability of a good or service. However, it is notoriously difficult to give hard and fast rules on this matter. The starting point certainly is the same as in English law: people do not have to share the information they have. Often this information is acquired through one's own efforts, by costly research, by training or by experience and the duty to give it away would gravely weaken the incentive of people to inform themselves before concluding a contract. The buyer therefore need not tell the seller about a likely surge of the market for a certain product, and the art collector can usually remain silent if he discovers a valuable painting at a flea market. But otherwise much depends on the exact circumstances of the case, including whether a party had special expertise, the cost of acquiring the relevant information and whether the other party could reasonably acquire the information for itself.[33] Only for some common situations is it clear what this leads to. A car dealer is supposed to give information about the safety of the used car he is selling because it would be much costlier for the non-professional buyer to inform himself. Most jurisdictions also hold that a layperson has to disclose the fact the house she is selling is constructed over a swamp – unless this is easy to discover by the buyer himself. Economists would reason that these nuanced rules avoid market failure. If, for example, the buyer of a used car does not have good information about its quality he runs the risk of buying a bad car (a 'lemon') and will therefore only be willing to pay an average price. This will drive away sellers of good cars, in the end leading to a 'market for lemons'.[34]

A second common source of disputes is how to interpret the terms of the agreement. For example, if a transport contract refers to 'delivery' one party may have in mind that the goods will be delivered by land, while the other thought of delivery by air. If a lease contract refers to a flat 'on the first floor', parties could argue about whether this is the first floor above the ground (the European meaning) or the ground floor (as in the United States). To say this is a matter of establishing the common intention of the parties is not very helpful, as this is precisely

---

what the parties argue about. The better position is therefore to interpret contract terms in the way in which a reasonable person would understand them. The law can do so in two fundamentally different ways. It can take the civil law approach and rely on the subjective intention of the parties as the starting point, meaning that it is decisive how a reasonable man in the position of the party would understand this intention. The law can also take the English approach and give preference to the objective meaning of the words, which focuses on 'what a reasonable person having all the background knowledge which would have been available to the parties would have understood them to be using the language in the contract to mean'.[35] On this view the natural and ordinary meaning of the clause will prevail. Again, both views reflect a different understanding of how much the law should help a slack party. English law puts a bonus on those who draft their agreement carefully, while a French or German party may benefit from the court's willingness to remedy sloppy drafting.

The third issue is whether a contract term can be set aside for reason of being unfair. It was already noted that contract law is impregnated with devices aiming to avoid so-called procedural unfairness. A contract is never only unfair because one party agrees to pay 'too much', but could be annulled if a party took advantage of the other party's needs, lack of experience, unfamiliarity with the subject matter of the contract or weak bargaining position.[36] However, practice shows that safeguarding procedural fairness may not be enough, particularly in the case of standard form contracts. Such contracts of adhesion contain conditions that are typically dictated by the stronger party and presented as 'take it or leave it'.[37] In the case of contracts entered into by consumers or small businesses it is also not very efficient if they would have to negotiate over the terms. The ensuing risk is that the terms are one-sided, for example by unduly limiting the buyer's right to damages or repair of the product. This is why legislators around the world have enacted specific rules to protect against substantive unfairness in general conditions. The European legislator, for example, allows courts to hold a standard clause invalid if 'contrary to the requirement of good faith, it causes a significant imbalance in the parties' rights and

---

35 *Chartbrook v Persimmon Homes* [2009] AC 1101 (HL) *per* Lord Hoffmann.
36 Cf. *Director General of Fair Trading v First National Bank* [2001] UKHL 52 (HL) *per* Lord Bingham.
37 Kessler 1943, 632.

obligations under the contract'.[38] Common law courts can reach similar results using the doctrine of unconscionability,[39] but seem increasingly reluctant to do so, possibly because of the belief that *ex ante* mandatory disclosure of terms (as discussed above) works better than *ex post* judicial control.

Contracts cannot only be a source of injustice among the contracting parties themselves but can also negatively affect third parties. For example, my decision to purchase a Volkswagen will make pollution increase to the detriment of many. And when I buy clothes at JCPenney or Primark it is not unlikely these were manufactured under questionable labour conditions in developing countries. A much-debated question is whether Western consumers or marginalised local workers could hold the Western retailer or garment company liable for human rights violations somewhere in the supply chain. This liability could be induced by a company's public declaration that it complies with a code for corporate social responsibility.[40] But even then courts find it difficult to step beyond the classical view of contracts only having legal effects among parties. We lack a convincing theory of how to accommodate harm done to others through contracting.[41] For example, the claim of employees of Wal-Mart's foreign suppliers in China, Bangladesh and Indonesia against Wal-Mart to improve local labour conditions in 'sweatshops' failed, even though Wal-Mart was eager to advertise on its home market that it only used responsible suppliers. A Californian court found it impossible to regard the employees as third-party beneficiaries of standards Wal-Mart obliged its suppliers to use.[42] It remains to be seen whether the increasing sensitivity of people to the cost of consumption as a result of issues like global warming, carbon footprints and business scandals will change this unadventurous view of the law.

2.5   Remedies and enforcement

The world would be in a bad state if the great majority of contracts concluded on a daily basis were not properly performed. The purchaser of a product usually pays the contract price and the employee typically

---

38 Art. 3 EU-Directive 93/13 on unfair terms in consumer contracts.

39 See, e.g., UCC § 2-302.

40 See, e.g., the 2011 UN Guiding Principles on Business and Human Rights.

41 Trebilcock 1993, 58 ff.

42 *Doe v Wal-Mart Stores*, 572 F.3d 677 (2009).

carries out the work with reasonable care and skill. But, although it is not normal that parties breach their contracts, the law must provide default rules balancing the interests of creditor and debtor for the case in which they do. The law on remedies for non-performance centres around three main questions: when is a party allowed to ask for performance, when can damages for breach be claimed, and when is a party entitled to terminate the contract?[43]

Before going into each of these three legal remedies, it is important to emphasise that litigation is not the only means to resolve contract disputes. Parties often resort to mediation, arbitration and other alternative mechanisms of dispute resolution, or decide simply to take their loss. This is particularly true in cases where the contract is only one element of a more complex relationship requiring continuous cooperation and sharing of benefits and burdens among the parties (as in the case of commercial leases, franchises or software agreements).[44] In these cases many parties will try to avoid having to go to state courts. The strategy of most commercial parties is simply not to rely *ex post* on the courts, which tend to be slow and expensive anyway, but to avoid disputes *ex ante*. They do so by contracting with parties that have a good reputation or from whom they have received some form of guarantee (e.g., in the form of pre-payment).[45] Thanks to the rise of the Internet, reputation no longer even needs to be based on experience or close social contacts. The reliability of perfect strangers can now be assessed through websites identifying bad payers or through online feedback mechanisms rating contracting parties.[46] If, even with the availability of these precautions, the creditor still falls victim to mal-performance he is likely to take his loss and spread the word about his unreliable counterpart, which probably serves as a more effective sanction than taking the debtor to court.[47]

This reality check should not conceal that legal enforcement remains important. The oft-discussed World Bank *Doing Business* reports regard fast and efficient dispute resolution by state courts as one of the main indicators for the success of a country's economy.[48] But here

---

43 Beale et al. 2010, 831 ff.
44 Macneil 1978 speaks of relational contracts.
45 Dietz 2014.
46 See, e.g., www.creditorwatch.com.au, eBay and Booking.com.
47 Macaulay 1963.
48 World Bank 2016.

one should not get one's hopes up too high. In the latest report New Zealand and Rwanda are ranked highest on this criterion, both taking a period of no more than ten months to enforce a contract through court proceedings (Bangladesh ranking lowest with four years). This is surely an incentive for commercial parties to resort to private arbitration while consumers would benefit greatly from dedicated small claims courts with informal hearings, simplified evidence rules and no mandatory representation. But even then it is unlikely that one individual consumer would bring a court action over the relatively small amount typically involved in a consumer case. Collective (or 'class') actions, in which consumers bring a joint lawsuit against the defendant, would work better but are still rare to find.

2.5.1   Performance

No one will enter into a contract without the expectation that at least the other party is going to perform its obligations. The law's interest lies with the pathological situation in which this expectation is disrupted. It could be that the purchased soybeans were never delivered, that the contractor is late in finishing the house he is to build or that the rock singer prefers to hang out with her friends instead of performing at the Olympic oval. The principle of binding force would mean very little if the law would not protect the expectations of the aggrieved parties in such cases of breach of contract. It does so by placing the creditor in the position it would have been in had the breaching party performed. The most obvious and easy way of doing this is to allow the creditor to force the debtor to perform *in natura*, by obtaining a court order for delivery of the soybeans or for the lazy contractor to finish the house. This claim for specific performance is the routine remedy in civil law jurisdictions, true to the idea that a contract is a moral device: promises must be kept.[49] Of course, the claim cannot be brought if performance has become impossible (hard to imagine in the case of commercial sales of generic goods) or depends entirely on the debtor's personal qualities (as in the above example: a judge cannot make an artist sing to the best of her ability), but otherwise the debtor can be forced to do what he promised.

Another way to protect the expectations of a commercial party is to allow him or her to claim monetary compensation. This is the position of the common law. If A agrees to sell 100 barrels of oil to B, and A

---

49 See, e.g., § 241 (1) BGB and Art. 1217 French *Code Civil.*

does not deliver, then why would B not be satisfied with damages? If A compensates B for the costs he incurred in concluding the contract as well as for the lost profits, A is prevented from having to find substitute goods to deliver to B while B obtains the money value of the contract. This is only different if a party has an interest in obtaining a specific good like a house or a rare painting, for which the common law indeed allows a claim for specific performance.[50] But in the case of products that are readily available on the market it is a commercially viable solution to leave the debtor the choice between performance and paying the expectation interest. The famous American jurist Oliver Wendell Holmes put it like this: '[t]he only universal consequence of a legally binding promise is, that the law makes the promisor pay damages if the promised event does not come to pass. In every case it leaves him free . . . to break his contract if he chooses'.[51] Because it is difficult to see how this argument could also apply to consumers – the buyer of a washing machine or an iPad is simply in need of the product itself for household use – the law entitles them to claim delivery and even repair or replacement of the product when needed.[52]

Sometimes a party argues that it is no longer able to perform because of extraordinary events that took place after the formation of the contract, but before the day of the agreed-upon performance. The law has no sympathy for the debtor's financial problems or for events he could have anticipated in a contractual 'hardship clause'. But what if the obstacle for performance is caused by a terrorist attack, a natural disaster or a sudden export restriction the parties had not reckoned on? Should a party be excused? Quite a few jurisdictions allow this if performance has become impracticable[53] or excessively onerous because of unforeseen circumstances.[54] These jurisdictions reason that a reasonable party would not hold the other to the contract, or that it must in any event be adapted to meet the changed situation. This doctrine found its most famous application in 1920s Germany, when inflation was proverbially high (at one point in time it took 4 billion German mark to buy one American dollar). The highest German court of that time (the *Reichsgericht*) had to decide on various occasions

---

50 See, e.g., s. 52 English Sales of Goods Act 1979 and Restatement (Second) of Contracts § 359 (1981).

51 Holmes 1881, 236.

52 See, e.g., EU-Directive 1999/44 on sale of consumer goods; US law often reaches a similar result through an implied warranty of merchantability of the sold goods.

53 Restatement (Second) of Contracts § 261 (1981) and UCC § 2-615.

54 See, e.g., § 313 BGB, Art. 1195 French *Code Civil* and Art. 6:111 PECL.

whether a debtor should be allowed to pay only the nominal value of a debt originated before the First World War – which would have meant he received the counter-performance practically for free. The court refused to allow this principle of 'Mark equals Mark' and even fixed new exchange rates, basing these revolutionary decisions on the good faith provision of § 242 BGB.[55]

English courts only allow a party to escape if the supervening event fundamentally changes the nature of the performance, which is extremely rare. Non-performance was allowed in the well-known decision in *Krell v Henry*, in which Henry had hired a room for two days to watch the procession for the coronation of King Edward VII. When Edward fell ill and the coronation was postponed, Henry refused to pay for the room. The court rejected Krell's claim for payment by holding that the purpose of the contract was frustrated: the coronation was so essential to the contract that parties were no longer bound when the coronation was cancelled.[56] But the overall reluctance of the English courts to help the debtor can be illustrated by an equally famous case in which the parties had agreed upon the shipping of 300 tons of Sudanese peanuts from Port Sudan to Hamburg. Both parties assumed that the ship could navigate through the Suez Canal, but shortly after the conclusion of the contract the Canal was blocked as a result of the second Arab–Israeli War of 1956. The shipment then had to go via the Cape of Good Hope, a distance three times longer than originally envisaged. The court did not find this a case of frustration and argued it was still possible to perform, even though more difficult and costly than anticipated.[57]

2.5.2   Damages for breach

A contract would be worth very little if the creditor did not have the right to claim damages if performance did not take place at all, was too late or was defective. As noted earlier, a breach of the contract allows the aggrieved party to be brought as much as possible to the position in which it would have been if the contract had been properly performed. Lawyers can argue endlessly about whether this expectation interest is indeed the proper interest that must be protected, or whether it should be the reliance or restitution interest, but this is

---

55 See, e.g., Reichsgericht 28 November 1923, RGZ 107, 78 (*Luderitzbucht Mortgage*).

56 *Krell v Henry* [1903] 2 KB 740 (CoA).

57 *Tsakiroglou Co Ltd v Noblee Thorl GmbH* [1962] AC 93 (HL).

not our main concern here.[58] When viewed from the perspective of how reasonable parties should behave, the more important question is when the damages claim should be available. There are two ways to reason about this.

The first is to hold the non-performing party liable simply because it did not perform. In this view, it does not matter whether the party was at fault or not: the mere fact of non-performance gives rise to a liability in damages. This is the position of the common law, captured in the English case of *Nicolene Ltd v Simmonds*: '[i]t does not matter whether the failure to fulfil the contract by the seller is because he is indifferent or wilfully negligent or just unfortunate. It does not matter what the reason is. What matters is the fact of performance. Has he performed or not?' Even if the information technology company could not help it that the network was down for more than a day, it still needs to compensate its customers. This view downplays the role of the debtor's individual fault.

The other way of reasoning is to allow a claim for damages only if the party in breach was at fault, or can at least be held responsible for the non-performance. This is the position of most civil law jurisdictions. Thus, Art. 1218 of the French Civil Code states that no damages are due when the person who is to perform was prevented from doing so by an irresistible force (so-called *force majeure*). This means that in most cases a party is freed from any liability if it can prove it exercised best efforts.

Despite these different mentalities of common law and civil law, both legal traditions come close in the practical results they reach. If the Rolling Stones hired Wembley stadium for a series of three concerts and the stadium was set on fire by Manchester United supporters before the first concert took place, the rock group could not claim any damages. An English court is likely to construe an implied condition according to which the parties are excused if performance becomes impossible through no fault of their own.[59] Many civil law jurisdictions make use of a similar fiction, but then hold the debtor *liable* even though there was no fault on his part. In the case of sale of goods they can do so by implying that the seller has given a guarantee or warranty of the goods being fit for purpose. The good reason for thus shifting the

---

58 Fuller and Perdue 1936.
59 Cf. *Taylor v Caldwell* [1863] 122 ER 309 (KB).

risk of insufficient product quality to the seller is that he typically has more information about the goods than the buyer. Even if the seller could not help it that the goods were not fit for purpose or in conformity with the given description, he is in a better position to carry the risk of non-conformity.

2.5.3   Termination of the contract

If the aggrieved party claims damages for breach instead of performance, that party still needs to perform its own obligations under the contract, which may not be what this party wants. If the creditor has lost all confidence in proper performance by his counterpart he will simply want to exit from the contract, meaning that he is no longer bound and, if he already performed himself, is allowed to claim back what was already rendered. What allows for this is the remedy of termination of the contract but this remedy is one of last resort and not something parties can seek lightheartedly. Parties conclude a contract to obtain performance and the decision prematurely to bring this contract to an end is usually a bitter disappointment. Most creditors will therefore prefer to postpone the moment of termination until it is absolutely certain that the debtor is unwilling or unable to perform. But once the situation is manifest, there is a very good reason why termination must be possible: in the typical bilateral contract, each of the parties only wants to perform because the other party is to perform as well. If the latter party is unable or unwilling to carry out its obligations, the equilibrium between the mutual performances would be destroyed if the creditor were not able to escape.

The task of the law, therefore, is to balance the interest of the aggrieved party in termination and the interest of the defaulting party in being allowed to still perform the contract. It is evident that the creditor has a legitimate interest to be able to terminate if the debtor is unable or unwilling to perform or has gone bankrupt. In this case, the creditor should be allowed to free himself and find another party to contract with. However, it is the rightful interest of the defaulting debtor not to treat every minor breach as justifying termination. If shop A orders 100 hand-made bags from manufacturer B, and B delivers 98 bags on time but announces that the remaining two are likely to come next week, this would surely form a legitimate reason for A to claim damages for delay (if he suffers any), but it would normally not allow him to terminate the entire contract. If it did, B would suffer a great detriment by losing all incurred expenses, as he is not able to sell the bespoke bags to somebody else. This is why termination is only allowed in respect of breaches that are sufficiently serious. The test for this is different in each jurisdiction. While English law holds that the breached contract term must be a 'condition', i.e., a term going to the root of the contract, German law only allows termination in the case of non-performance of a main obligation or after the granting of an additional period to perform. The CISG and the PECL require a 'fundamental' non-performance.[60] Again, it is essential for the role that contract law assigns to party autonomy that these restrictive default rules can be overridden by a termination clause in the contract itself.

2.6   Contract as empowerment

Contract law provides the means for people to pursue what they value in life in the face of the equally valid claims of everyone else to do likewise.[61] Not state-made legislation but the private agreement mediates between the parties' conflicting interests. This focus on agreement as a source of obligations has proven a powerful metaphor, also outside of private law. Many political writers, ranging from Hobbes and Locke to Rousseau and Rawls, have used the image of the social contract to argue that the authority of the state derives from the (real or hypothetical) consent of the governed and not from God or nature. This contractarian model also forms the basis for the international law of treaties, which has copied all of its instruments from contract law, including capacity, binding force and good faith execution, interpretation, defects of consent and termination for non-performance.[62] Contract also provided the fresh thinking necessary to understand the functioning of companies. In a view of the firm as a nexus of contracts, a corporation is seen as a group of diverse actors (shareholders, managers, employees, customers and creditors) with a common goal tied together by a diverse set of voluntary exchanges.[63] Finally, the contract metaphor can even be used to make people do things that will never be enforceable in a court of law. For example, it is not uncommon for parents to 'contract' with their children about their behaviour online. Websites provide pre-formulated clauses parents can ask their children to sign, such as 'I will never agree to get together with someone I "meet" online

---

60 Arts. 25 CISG and 8:103 PECL.
61 Gutmann 2013, 48; Dagan 2015, 3.
62 Vienna Convention on the Law of Treaties 1969, respectively Arts. 6, 26, 31, 48–52 and 60.
63 Jensen 1998, 135.

without first checking with my parents'.[64] This is just another example of how 'contract' can empower people even outside of the marketplace.

Also in a more narrow understanding of enforceable agreements a bewildering variety of contract types exist: commercial and consumer; domestic and cross-border; contracts concluded on location, face-to-face or online; one-time sales contracts and long-term employment contracts; a gift to one's children and a €100 billion merger. The law's propensity is to provide general rules for all of these different contracts, even though they operate in highly diverse social settings and have very different economic goals. What does the employment contract, whose terms are typically set by collective bargaining and which provides the employee with the necessary means to live, have in common with the company takeover, other than a loose reference to the parties' consent? It may therefore be misguided to refer to contract law as one set of unifying principles. Perhaps only one principle firmly stands the test of reality: contracts empower people to meet their needs and desires, even if the contents of the contract are often set by others.

---

64 See, e.g., www.safekids.com.

3 Tort law

3.1 Introduction

Misfortune comes in many guises. Some people are born with a disability or contract a disease later in life, others suffer from hunger, have a bad love life, get hurt in a car crash or find it difficult to make ends meet. One only needs to consult a news website or watch a random episode of a television soap series to realise that tragedy is an indispensable part of the human condition. There is not much private law can do about this, except in a handful of well-defined situations that qualify as a *tort*. The law of torts (sometimes called the law of delict) responds to wrongs for which somebody else (the tortfeasor) can be held responsible. This limits the law's interference with individual misfortune to those cases in which the victim can point at one particular wrongdoer who caused the damage. The difference between A, who is missing a leg since her birth as a result of some hereditary disease and B, who is missing a leg as a result of a car accident, is that B may still be lucky enough to be entitled to claim compensation from the negligent driver, while A is not.

A typical tort claim is therefore one in which the claimant can argue that the defendant wrongfully caused damage to him. A bystander punched in the face, a pedestrian hit by a driver, a house owner suffering from the neighbours' enduring noise, a celebrity whose privacy is invaded by a tabloid and a factory deprived of electricity as a result of a contractor cutting a cable while digging up a road may all be entitled to damages claiming the defendant should have treated them differently. It is important to realise that in each of these cases it is the *claimant* who makes this claim: he exercises his autonomy in deciding to hold the defendant liable and claim compensation.[1] This is where tort law differs from criminal law. Although some types of conduct (e.g., assault or drunk driving injuring somebody else) could both qualify as a crime

---

1 Tort law empowers by providing an avenue of civil recourse: Goldberg and Zipursky 2010.

and a tort, the victim does not hold the power to prosecute the suspect and have him fined or imprisoned for the sake of the public good. This is a power exclusively vested in the state. What the victim can do, however, is claim monetary compensation for the loss resulting from the defendant's behaviour.

This chapter examines some of the recurrent themes of today's tort law. The central question in this field is when behaviour is tortious and when it is not. It is certainly a fundamental principle of the law that wrongdoers are liable to pay damages to their victims but this leaves open what exactly constitutes a wrongdoing (Section 3.2). In addition, most modern jurisdictions accept that in some well-defined cases it is not even necessary to prove a wrongdoing by the defendant because he is held liable for another reason than being at fault (Section 3.3). Once it is established that the victim can hold the tortfeasor liable, the question emerges as to which aims a claim for damages serves to achieve (Section 3.4) and whether the damages can be said to have been caused by the wrong (Section 3.5). One final critical question is about alternatives to tort law and what its future may bring (Section 3.6).

3.2   Fault liability

The essential question of tort law is whether another person can be held liable for the losses somebody else has suffered. The usual answer is that this is exceptional: the victim bears the damage himself unless a special reason exists to pass it on to another person. Modern-day society, which emphasises people's responsibility for their own actions, finds this special reason first and foremost in _fault_. The typical tort action is one in which the claimant asserts the defendant did something wrong either because he wrongfully _intended_ to cause damage or because he was _negligent_ in doing so. It follows from this that many a loss is not recoverable in law. If I drink my coffee or do my shopping at a place other than the one I am used to, my old café or store will unquestionably suffer economic damage but the law does not consider my actions as wrong. The underlying rationale for this is that if I were held liable it would place too much of a restriction on my autonomy in choosing the place I want to spend my money. Lord Atkin famously put it like this in the case of *Donoghue v Stevenson*:

> [A]cts or omissions which any moral code would censure cannot in a practical world be treated so as to give a right to every person injured by them to

demand relief . . . The rule that you are to love your neighbour becomes in law, you must not injure your neighbour.[2]

Tort law must therefore establish which behaviour falls short of the minimal duties the law forces citizens to adopt towards one another. National legislators and highest courts provide guidance on this, be it in different ways. French law, for example, provides only one norm for fault liability. The famous general clause of Art. 1240 French Civil Code succinctly states: '[a]ny act of a person which causes harm to another obliges him by whose fault the damage occurred to make compensation for it'.[3] In an effort to curtail the freedom of the courts in holding people liable, the German Civil Code offers three main criteria: one for intentionally, or negligently, unlawfully injuring a life, body, health, freedom, property or another right of another person (§ 823-1 BGB), one for acting against a statute intended to protect another person (§ 823-2 BGB) and one for intentionally inflicting (economic) damage *contra bonos mores* on somebody else (§ 826 BGB). The common law is wary of accepting such general principles as to when behaviour is tortious and instead makes use of different heads of liability, each having their own detailed requirements and consequences – much in the same way as criminal law defines different crimes. Thus, next to the tort of negligence (in practice by far the most important category), the common law recognises more than 70 nominate torts ranging from trespass, assault, battery and nuisance to libel, slander and false imprisonment. If there is anything coming close to a more general principle of tort liability in English law it is negligence, which requires the damage to have been caused by a defendant who breached the duty of care he had towards the claimant.

These differences in national styles should not obscure the fact that tort laws around the world reason in similar ways when holding tortfeasors liable. Apart from the straightforward case in which the damage is caused intentionally (punching someone in the face or deliberately raising the volume of one's audio to irritate the neighbours), the ultimate criterion for fault liability is whether the defendant has failed to exercise reasonable care. It must be that he did not act in the way to be expected from a reasonably careful person in the position of the defendant in the circumstances of the case. Although this may sound like a terribly vague standard, it does allow courts to reach outcomes that are in sync

---

2 [1932] AC 580 (HL).
3 Art. 1382 until the reform through Ordonnance 2016-131.

with societal views of what is the desirable behaviour of people. Thus, a house owner is liable for injuries of invited guests if they slip on the snow-covered steps outside or are hit by a rotten tree, a doctor is liable when operating on the wrong patient because of misreading the chart, a constructor is liable for a falling crane if he did not sufficiently secure it and a football club unwilling to body-check supporters before entering the stadium is liable for injuries to spectators. Each of the defendants in these examples failed to do something that a reasonable person would have done in the same situation as they were in.

Not many will disagree with the outcome of the above examples.[4] However, it seems highly unsatisfactory that these decisions could be based only on the criterion: 'be careful'. Using such an open-ended standard also runs the risk of expanding the range of tort liability too far. The constant struggle in tort law is to provide compensation where reasonable and yet avoid an unlimited liability, as this would have a chilling effect on social and commercial intercourse. English law nicely illustrates this struggle. Lord Atkin's criterion for negligence in *Donoghue v Stevenson* greatly expanded the circle of potential tortfeasors when he wrote:

> You must take reasonable care to avoid acts or omissions which you can reasonably foresee would be likely to injure your neighbour. Who, then, in law is my neighbour? The answer seems to be – persons who are so closely and directly affected by my act that I ought reasonably to have them in contemplation as being so affected when I am directing my mind to the acts or omissions which are called in question.

The case law of the English courts in the 80 years thereafter is one huge attempt to (first) expand and (later) restrict the realm of this 'neighbour principle'.[5] However, the truth of the matter may well be that any reference to phrases as general as reasonableness, wrongfulness, duty, or proximity will never grasp the 'real' motivation for holding someone liable, which may be much more influenced by some rough situation sense.

This is no reason to be sceptical about the coherence of tort law. In practice courts tend to use a variety of well-established factors in

---

4 Of which the first and the last were actually decided by courts: Reichsgericht 23 February 1903, RGZ 54, 53 and Cour d'appel de Lyon 16 December 1988, JCP 1990.II.21510.

5 Weir 2006, 29 ff; *Caparo Industries plc v Dickman* [1990] 2 AC 605 (HL).

deciding about fault liability. This can be illustrated by reference to so-called 'slip-and-fall' cases. These are common types of accidents in which someone gets injured as a result of slipping on, for example, a wet floor in a restaurant or a lettuce leaf in a store.[6] The question of whether the defendant has failed to exercise reasonable care is then answered by considering factors such as how likely it is that people will not be prudent at the place of the accident, how probable it is for accidents to occur as a result, how severe the consequences of the accident can be and how difficult it is to take preventive measures. In the American case of *United States v Carroll Towing Co* judge Learned Hand put this into an algebraic formula: if the probability of an accident is called P, the injury L and the burden of precautions B, liability depends on whether B is less than L multiplied by P, i.e. whether $B<PL$.[7] This provides an economic justification of liability as it takes away money from those who do not take cost-justified precautions. If in a slip-and-fall case it would have been easy for the defendant to avoid injuring people (e.g., place a sign 'caution: wet floor') he is more likely to be liable than in the case where it would have been very costly to do so.

Case law provides illustrations of how this multi-factor approach can be extended to other cases of endangering people. In the English case of *Bolton v Stone*, a Miss Stone, standing outside her house during a game of cricket taking place at the nearby grounds, claimed damages from the cricket club when she was hit on the head by a ball.[8] The club was not held liable: the grounds had been fenced off and the road outside the grounds was not very busy. Sufficient precautions had therefore been taken to reduce the risk of accident. The grounds should have been roofed or surrounded by a higher fence to avoid accidents, but this would have been disproportional in view of the very small risk that someone could get hurt. This case can be contrasted with the recent decision of a Connecticut federal district court in *Munn v Hotchkiss School*.[9] Fifteen-year-old Cara Munn was bitten by a tick while on a summer trip to China organised by her school. She contracted encephalitis, which left her unable to speak for the rest of her life. The victim argued the school had failed adequately to warn students of the risk of being infected and had not taken adequate

6 OLG Hamm 26 October 1981, *VersR* 1983, 43.

7 159 F 2d 169 (2d Cir. 1947).

8 [1951] 1 All ER 1078 (HL).

9 No. 3:2009cv00919 – Document 177 (D. Conn. 2013).

precautions against insect-borne disease before and during the trip. Although the risk of permanently losing one's speech as a result of a tick bite may be small, it would have been easy for the school to take protective measures, for example by urging students to use insect repellent, to wear proper clothing and to check themselves for ticks after returning to the hotel. The jury held the school liable. An extra argument for this is that, unlike Miss Stone and the cricket club, the victim stood in a special relationship to the defendant: schools owe a higher duty of care to their students than to strangers, as physicians have a special responsibility towards their patients, employers towards their employees and a chemical plant towards nearby farmers.

The great strength of using the yardstick of the reasonable person (or more colourful, though less gender-neutral, equivalents such as the man on the Clapham omnibus[10] and the *bonus paterfamilias*) is that the tortfeasor cannot argue that *he* was not the reasonably well-informed and normally diligent person the law wants him to be. It does not matter that the shop owner in a slip-and-fall case had a bad day, was depressed, hurt at his arm preventing him from cleaning up, or simply believed an accident would not occur. Also, the diligence expected from a learner-driver is the same as that required from a qualified driver in the same way as the mal-performing doctor, lawyer and teacher are judged by what their reasonable colleague would have done. Reversely, the victim cannot argue the tortfeasor in question was more capable than others: Sebastian Vettel and Max Verstappen do not owe their victims a higher standard than the average driver when causing an accident on the public road just because they are Formula 1 drivers. The test of negligence is thus an objective one: it does not take into account the characteristics, weaknesses or superiority of the parties in the case at hand. One compelling reason for this is that neither claimant nor defendant should be allowed unilaterally to set the applicable standard of care themselves.

The principle to hold someone only liable when he is at fault is clearly hard to reconcile with the aim of compensating victims. It fits the nineteenth-century age of liberalism and expanding capitalism to assume liability only in the rare case of when a loss is the result of somebody else's fault. One author therefore qualified fault liability as nothing but

---

10 On which recently, *Healthcare at Home Limited v The Common Services Agency* [2014] UKSC 49, 1–4.

a smokescreen to protect the interests of companies.[11] Today, society believes many cases exist in which the victim must be compensated even though the tortfeasor was not at fault. The most obvious instances of this we find in cases of no-fault or strict liability (discussed in Section 3.3) but the wish to protect victims also has its bearing upon the notion of fault itself. Nowadays negligence is often deemed to exist in cases in which there is not really any personal blame. Atiyah has called this the 'stretching effect of sympathy': the defendant may have done nothing wrong morally, but is still held liable.[12] One case in English law, that accepts liability for traffic accidents only in the case of negligence, was about a 75-year-old man who was unaware of the fact he had had a stroke a few minutes before he began to drive and subsequently caused an accident. He was held liable, no doubt influenced by the fact that drivers have mandatory liability insurance and therefore do not have to pay the damage themselves.[13] In one Dutch case a deer suddenly appeared on the road and the driver, forced to decide in a split second, steered his car into the other lane where he collided with another vehicle. Even though it is quite understandable of the driver to have made the wrong choice (the average driver could have acted in a similar way), the defendant was liable.[14]

A further illustration of attributing fault is when a tortfeasor acts under the influence of a mental or physical disability. This is quite acceptable in the instance where the defendant knows about his own frailty: the blind, the deaf and the physically disabled must meet the same standard of care as anyone else when participating in society. This is also true in the case of a temporary disorder caused by using alcohol or drugs because the tortfeasor has deliberately put himself into this position and must bear the consequences thereof. But also in cases where the disability is completely unexpected many jurisdictions are willing to assume responsibility inspired by the wish to protect the victim. When one Erma Veith believed God had taken hold of the steering wheel and He veered her car into the plaintiff's lane, Erma could not plead she was under a mental delusion to escape liability.[15] The American Restatement (Third) of Torts § 11 (c) puts it like this: '[a]n actor's mental or emotional disability is not considered in

---

11 Horwitz 1977, 85.
12 Atiyah 1997, 36.
13 *Roberts v Ramsbottom* [1980] 1 WLR 823 (QB).
14 Hoge Raad 11 November 1983, NJ 1984, 331 (*Lanting/DLG*).
15 *Breunig v American Family Insurance Co*, 173 NW 2d 619 (1970).

determining whether conduct is negligent, unless the actor is a child'. This is no longer a matter of how people should treat each other but simply a policy decision about whose problem it is when things go wrong.

One special type of liability must be mentioned here, although it is not truly a fault liability of the liable person. This is the so-called vicarious liability of employers for acts of their employees. If a security guard on duty carelessly throws away a burning cigarette causing a fire to the building he is supposed to protect, he is indubitably liable in fault himself. Interestingly, the law also makes his employer liable, regardless of whether he carefully selected, trained and supervised the employee: the employer simply has to answer for the torts of his staff. Most jurisdictions accept this principle of *respondeat superior*[16] arguing that vis-à-vis third parties acts of the employee can be considered as acts of the employer, at least in so far as they are carried out in the exercise of the functions assigned to him. Employees are in this sense nothing but the extended arm of the employer himself: their fault creates his liability. Thus, the taxi company is vicariously liable for the accidents caused by its drivers and the church is liable for sexual abuse by its priests.[17] In the background lurk the arguments of insurance (the cost of liability must be borne by those who can more easily insure against it) and of the victim's need to find a solvent party: the employer tends to have deeper pockets than the employee. This, of course, must not be a licence for the employee to be careless: apart from the simple incentive of not being fired, the employee himself usually remains liable next to the employer, allowing the victim to choose from whom he wants to claim his losses.

3.3   Strict liability

It was noted above that the law finds a good reason to shift a loss when the person causing it is at fault even though courts may sometimes stretch fault in order to give compensation. In some well-defined cases, however, the law openly makes people pay damages regardless of fault. Such a no-fault (or 'strict') liability is invariably based on the fact that the tortfeasor acts in a certain capacity in which he has to answer for the damage caused by dangerous persons or things under his control

---

16 The most notable exception being the – heavily criticised – § 831 BGB.
17 *Doe v Bennett*, 2004 SCC 17 (Supreme Court of Canada).

or by dangerous activities he deploys. With a capacity comes responsibility. This explains why, in particular, strict liabilities are put on persons who profit from the danger they create and who are able to insure against it. Two types of dangers deserve the law's special attention.[18]

The first type of strict liability exists for inherently dangerous people, goods or activities. These retain their uncontrollable energy even if treated, stored or handled with the greatest possible care. Although the use of railways, automobiles, nuclear energy, hazardous chemicals, explosives and gas are potentially highly dangerous, society cannot do without. The law therefore does not prohibit their use, but it does assume liability if any damage results from it. Using dynamite to destroy a building is perfectly fine as long as the neighbour is compensated for the debris causing damage to his nearby house. The American Restatement (Second) of Torts captures this idea as follows: '[o]ne who carries on an abnormally dangerous activity is subject to liability for harm to the person, land, or chattels of another resulting from the activity, although he has exercised the utmost care to prevent the harm'.[19] With this form of liability the reasonable person standard could not be further away.

The rise of modern strict liability finds its origins in industrialisation and the risks it creates. Early examples are special statutes (first in Prussia in 1838, soon followed by other jurisdictions) to compensate victims of railway accidents, but, practically, the acceptance of liability of employers for industrial accidents towards the end of the nineteenth century was much more important. In many a country it would be unthinkable today that the worker who lost a limb while at work would have the burden of providing the difficult proof of an employer's fault, but it took a long time before this was accepted. The famous campaign slogan in Britain of the 1890s was: 'the cost of the product should bear the blood of the workman'.[20] This hits the nail on the head because it highlights that the employer is in a much better position to spread the costs of the accident (by insuring himself and by raising the price of the product) than the individual victim. Another way to deal with this is to introduce social insurance for industrial accidents, a solution adopted in Germany in the 1880s and later in many other countries as well. Meanwhile, the pendulum is shifting back. Thus, the United Kingdom

---

18 Epstein 1973, 177 ff.
19 Restatement (Second) of Torts § 519 (1) (1965).
20 Prosser 1984, 573.

recently removed the standard of strict liability for the violation of certain health and safety regulations in an effort to combat the 'compensation culture'. It is no longer seen as fair and just to hold employers liable when they took all reasonable steps to prevent the accident.[21] This also seems to fit better modern working life, where the risk is often no longer that of physical injury but of mental distress caused by too high stress levels at the working place. To avoid this from happening is a joint responsibility of employer and employee.

Apart from the risk of accidents at the workplace, another important source of danger in today's society consists of participating in traffic, either as a motorist or as a pedestrian or cyclist. Motor vehicles are undoubtedly inherently dangerous objects that, even if the driver exercises utmost care, can cause grievance. Lord Denning put it like this:

> [A]ny civilised system of law should require, as a matter of principle, that the person who uses this dangerous instrument on the roads – dealing with death and destruction all around – should be liable to make compensation to anyone who is killed or injured in consequence of the use of it.[22]

Interestingly, however, only a few jurisdictions accept a full strict liability for traffic accidents. English law certainly does not: it bases traffic liability still on negligence by asking whether the driver breached his duty to exercise reasonable care not to injure anyone else. French law, with a strict liability of motorists versus pedestrians and cyclists who suffer personal injury, is at the other end of the spectrum. However, such differences between national regimes of traffic liability do not really affect the position of the injured party because many countries have compulsory insurance against the risk of liability for accidents caused by motor vehicles. This is both in the interest of the victim (who is certain to be compensated) and of the motorist-tortfeasor (who will not go bankrupt in case of an accident). Routine cases of personal injury in the case of automobile accidents – in fact the bulk of tort cases in any legal system – are therefore usually dealt with among private insurers.

Not only goods or activities are inherently dangerous. This is also true for a special category of people, namely young children. Their impul-

---

21 Enterprise and Regulatory Reform Act 2013, amending s. 47 of the Health and Safety at Work Act 1984.
22 Denning 1982, 128.

siveness and ability to cause damage, even when parents exercise the highest possible care to avoid this, merits to put them into the same category as ultra-hazardous goods and activities. They also fit this category because there is a societal need to allow children to grow up and they cannot be kept from risk while doing so. It is not impossible that the child itself would be liable in fault – although difficult to imagine in a case where the child has not yet reached the age of discretion (and is thus unable to distinguish between right and wrong) – but strict liability must in any event rest upon the parents. If a five year old kicks a ball through the neighbour's window her parents will have to answer for this. However, this result is not reached in all jurisdictions, which in fact show a great variety in their approaches of dealing with this issue. Dutch and French law make parents strictly liable for acts of their children (below the age of 14 in Dutch law and below the age of 18 if still living with their parents (Art. 1242-4 French Civil Code) in French law), while German law adopts a rebuttable presumption of negligence (§ 832 BGB) allowing the parents to prove they sufficiently supervised the child. What sufficient supervision means will depend on the age and character of the minor: generally speaking, the older the child the less supervision it needs. English law simply requires negligence.

The second type of strict liability exists for products or things that are not inherently dangerous but turn out defective for the purpose they were designed for. There is nothing inherently dangerous in a building, a mobile phone or a breast implant but if they collapse, explode or leak they were – in hindsight – apparently not safe enough for their intended use. In these types of cases, however, it is often highly difficult for the victim to prove fault. He cannot easily prove whether the collapse of a building was caused by a defective design or insufficient maintenance or which precautions the manufacturer took to ensure the safety of the product. This, again together with the argument that the tortfeasor can easily insure against liability, are good reasons to reverse the burden of proof or even establish strict liability. Product liability is a prime example of the latter. Both in Europe and in the United States the manufacturer who sends out defective products into the world is held strictly liable for the injuries and material damage resulting therefrom. In Europe this is the result of EU-directive 85/374 of which Art. 1 crisply states: '[t]he producer shall be liable for damage caused by a defect in his product' (be it truncated by many restrictions in the subsequent provisions). The American Restatement puts it like this: '[o]ne engaged in the business of selling or otherwise distributing products who sells or distributes a defective product is subject to liability for harm to persons or property caused by the defect'.[23] Upon reading these provisions the realm of this liability is potentially unlimited: baby blankets may make a baby choke, condoms may leak, a car may have too little breaking power, a medicine may be poisonous, an electric tea kettle may cause a fire and sunglasses may not offer enough protection against UV-radiation. However, much depends on what is considered 'defective'. If a product is defective when it does not provide the safety which a person is entitled to expect (as both Art. 6 of the EU-directive and the Restatement hold), the reasonable person makes a glorious comeback in the form of the sufficiently diligent manufacturer. This means that not just any defective blanket, condom or sunglasses make the manufacturer automatically liable.[24] For example, the exploding bottle striking a random visitor of a pub invites the question how diligent the manufacturer of the bottle should have been: all that can be asked for is that he took all necessary precautions to make the bottle meet the required safety level.

It is inevitable for national jurisdictions to show marked differences in the extent to which they accept strict liability. It fits the above to say that English law is the most cautious, while French law goes furthest. In its famous *Jand'heur* decision of 1930 the highest court in France accepted a general liability for damage caused by things under one's control, even if these things are not dangerous in themselves (such as basketballs, pedals, skis and chairs).[25] However, it was also noted that legislators and courts may sneak remnants of the reasonable person into strict liabilities. This is not only true for product liability but also for the somewhat idiosyncratic liability of the keeper of animals. And now that an objective standard is applied in fault liability, the truth of the matter is that the various types of liability form a sliding scale.

3.4   Compensation and deterrence: on remedies in tort law

It has by now become abundantly clear that tort law does two things: it sets norms for behaviour by requiring people to act as reasonable persons *and* it makes people liable for damage caused by dangerous activities society finds legitimate. In both instances tort law selects the

---

23 Restatement (Third) of Torts: Products Liability § 1 (1997).
24 Cf. Wagner 2006, 1032.
25 Art. 1242-1 French *Code Civil* and Cass. 13 February 1930, p 1930.I.121 (*Jand'heur*).

cases in which the victim is empowered to recover from the tortfeasor. So far nothing has been said about the type of remedies the claimant can bring. The answer to this depends to a large extent on the aims one believes remedies in tort law should have: should a claim primarily compensate the victim for the suffered loss, should it deter the wrong-doer (and possibly others) from acting in the same way in the future, should it punish the tortfeasor, or, finally, should it simply serve to recognise that the defendant did something wrong?[26]

It is intuitive that a remedy in tort law serves, in any event, to com-pensate the victim for his losses. The tortfeasor has disturbed the existing equilibrium and must therefore restore the status quo by put-ting the victim as much as possible back into the position he would have been in had the tort not occurred. If corrective justice ever has a place in law, it is here: it allows the victim to get even. However, if making good the loss was the only aim of remedies in tort, better methods exist. Tort law is in fact a highly inefficient instrument to repair harm, because it requires individual victims to go through the slow and expensive justice system to get compensated. Social security and private insurance are both cheaper and quicker and may therefore be preferred over tort law.[27] This is why deterrence is often seen as another aim: the threat of liability in damages would stimulate the potential injurer not to commit a tort. If the reasonably careful John slips and falls on a wet floor in Anna's deli, John cannot do much to avoid this but Anna could have taken the necessary precautions to make John's accident less likely to occur. However, one may ask whether people are truly motivated to be more careful out of fear for a damages claim. In so far as being more or less careful is based on a rational decision about possible legal consequences at all, the fear of losing customers or of social sanctions is likely to play a bigger role. Certainly for companies and government bodies, fear of bad public-ity is a better incentive to obey the law than the risk of having to pay damages. As the saying goes: sunlight is the best of disinfectants. Moreover, it was noted earlier that tort law also holds people liable in cases where they are not really to blame but the damage is the simple result of an error or a brief moment of inattentiveness; criminal law, which usually requires intent, may do a better job in providing the appropriate incentive not to harm others.

26 Cf. Van Dam 2013, no. 1201-1-3.
27 This argument is forcefully made by Atiyah 1997.

A third possible function of a claim in tort law is to punish the tortfeasor for his wrongful behaviour. It can do so by awarding a greater sum of damages than the actual loss suffered by the victim. This legal technique can already be found in the Old Testament, which utters: '[i]f a man shall steal an ox, or a sheep, and kill it, or sell it, he shall restore five oxen for an ox, and four sheep for a sheep'.[28] Not many jurisdictions are willing to accept this wisdom, but those that do attract a lot of attention. American law in particular provides well-known examples of juries willing to award high amounts of punitive damages in cases of intentional or reckless wrongdoing. In *Liebeck v McDonald's*[29] an elderly lady spilled McDonald's coffee onto her lap resulting in severe burns on her thighs, buttocks and genitals. The jury awarded $2.7 million in punitive damages, later reduced by the appeals judge to $480,000. The publicity these cases attract is not representative of American law as a whole. Only in 2 per cent of civil cases are punitive damages awarded and the average amount does not exceed $50,000. However, in non-frivolous cases punitive damages can fulfil a highly useful function in preventing companies from future wrongful behaviour, as demonstrated by the case of *Grimshaw v Ford Motor Company*.[30] The gas tank in Lily Gray's Ford Pinto exploded when her car was struck from behind by another vehicle. Lily died and her 13-year-old son Richard was severely burned. It turned out that the gas tank in other cars of the same type also tended to explode when involved in a rear-end collision as a result of a faulty design of the car. Ford knew about this defect before it put the Pinto on the market but considered it too expensive to do anything about it. The company had rationally calculated that to remedy the mechanical problem would have cost over $100 million ($11 per car) while the likely costs of claims by possible victims were estimated at only $50 million. The jury had no trepidation in awarding $125 million in punitive damages to Richard. Although this amount was reduced by the court, it is clear that in cases like these punitive damages can be an effective means of deterring a company from entering into such outrageous conduct again. However, this is not an argument likely to be swallowed in Europe: the main reason why hardly any European jurisdiction allows punitive damages is because they believe an individual claimant would then act as a 'private attorney general' thus going against the state monopoly on punishment.

---

28 Exodus 22:1.

29 *Liebeck v McDonald's Restaurants*, No. D-202 CV-93-02419, 1995 WL 360309 (Bernalillo County, New Mexico Dist. Ct. 18 August 1994).

30 119 Cal.App.3d 757.

A final aim of pursuing a remedy in tort law is the judicial recognition of a wrong. Many victims, who will often be compensated by insurance anyway, are not after money but find it more important that 'justice is done'. They want a court to state the defendant was wrong. The defendant making a public apology would be even better, but this is not something the court can oblige a party to do. What the claimant can ask for, however, is a declaration of rights or a symbolic amount of damages of, say, €1 (so-called nominal damages or a *franc symbolique*). A legal procedure is then a way to make the defendant publicly accountable and provide publicity about the wrongs he committed. If a hospital is liable for medical malpractice by its doctors, or a public body is liable for corruption, judicial recognition of these wrongs can help both victims and society to get answers. In this sense, tort law can also have a therapeutic value. Attempts to get to grips with the distant past, such as the recent attempts of a number of Caribbean states to bring European countries to justice for the part they played in the slave trade, must also be seen in this light.

None of these four aims alone can explain why committing a tort should allow the claimant to bring legal action. When taken together, however, they provide convincing arguments for why violation of a norm of tort law allows a claim for damages, an injunction (preventing imminent damage to occur) or a declaration of rights. In practice, a claim for damages is the action that is brought most. In line with its compensatory function, it is aimed at the full reparation of the claimant's losses. This includes compensation of damaged property, of the costs caused by the accident and of lost expectations. If A's car is wrecked in an accident for which B is responsible, B has to compensate A with an amount enabling him to repair the car or buy an equivalent one. If A was hurt, he can also claim compensation of the costs caused by the accident, such as his medical expenses, costs of transport to the hospital, costs of adapting a house or of hiring help, etc. In addition, if as a result of his injuries A is no longer able to work, B will also have to make good his lost expectations, in particular lost income. It is in this respect unfortunate for the tortfeasor that a golden rule of tort law is that he has to take the victim as he finds him: if the victim happens to be the Chief Executive Officer (CEO) of a big company, he will be liable for a much higher amount than in the case of hitting a retired window washer.

A different type of action is to claim damages for pain and suffering. This is aimed at compensation for non-material harm. Such harm cannot really be made good by money, but money can help the victim to obtain a substitute for his loss or offer comfort for what happened.[31] If A is an avid runner and loses his leg as a result of the defendant's tort, money is not going to bring back his leg but it can help A to find some other form of pleasure. This is why the law generally accepts a claim for pain and suffering in the case of physical injury, though certainly not only in that case. Courts around the world have also awarded such damages in cases of false imprisonment, disturbance by neighbours, lost holiday pleasure and unjustified dismissal by employers. The problem with non-pecuniary damages, however, is that the loss is not measurable in a market. This makes it impossible objectively to evaluate the suffering. Some jurisdictions therefore set a cap on this type of damage (e.g., several American state legislatures limit the amount in most cases to $800,000, also out of fear juries would award higher sums). Other jurisdictions rely on charts reflecting the courts' awards for damages in concrete cases.

Damages for pain and suffering find a highly important application in the case of infringement of so-called personality rights. Tort law protects not only what people have but also what people are, that is their *being*. Peoples' economic interests may differ widely dependent on how much money and assets they have but every person, no matter how poor or deprived, has the right to life, bodily integrity, honour and reputation. These rights exist due to the sole fact of being a person, which is why they are sometimes called *private human rights*: rights so fundamental that they cannot only be enforced against the state but also vis-à-vis other citizens. In the last century, courts have greatly expanded the scope of such personality rights. For example, they have granted adopted children the right to know their birth parents and patients the right to inspect their own medical files. Courts have also awarded claims for pain and suffering in cases of sexual abuse, discrimination and failed sterilisation. For example, if Bank A refuses to provide a loan to client B on the basis of B's ethnicity, B is forced to enter into a contract with another bank, Y, under less beneficial conditions. B can then claim damages for economic loss from A (the difference between the cost of the loan by A and the cost of the loan by Y), but B may also be able to claim damages for pain and suffering because of violation of his dignity. In the same vein, if parents bring a claim against a hospital for recovery of the costs of pregnancy and childbirth (or even for the costs of raising the child) after a failed vasectomy, the

---

31 Cane 2013, 407 ff.

law has every reason to allow non-pecuniary damages. The parents have lost the opportunity to live their lives in the way they wished and planned, which is an important aspect of their personal autonomy, in this case the freedom to limit the size of their family.[32]

One of the most prominent personality rights is the right to protection of one's private life. The right to privacy was 'invented' by Warren and Brandeis in a celebrated law review article published in 1890.[33] Their plea in favour of a right 'to be let alone' has resonated around the world, leading to celebrated provisions such as Art. 9 of the French Civil Code ('Everyone has the right to respect for his private life'), Art. 8 ECHR and § 652A of the American Restatement (Second) of Torts ('One who invades the right of privacy of another is subject to liability for the resulting harm to the interests of the other').

The right to private life is never absolute. It must always be balanced against other interests, such as the right to freedom of expression and press. One of the few assets of European royalty is that they are a great source of case law on how to weigh these interests. In one authoritative case, Princess Caroline of Monaco complained about the publication of paparazzi photos taken of her while she was shopping and dining with her then partner. The claim she brought against the tabloid magazine failed before the German courts, which, true to a long-standing tradition, distinguished between private and public figures. Public figures, as 'persons of contemporary history', would have to accept publication of photos when taken in public spaces.[34] However, this broad protection of the free press was set aside by the European Court of Human Rights[35] for violation of Art. 8 ECHR. The Strasbourg court argued that celebrities also have a right to privacy when leaving their home unless they act in an official function or when the watchdog function of the press essential to a democratic society is at stake. The mere goal of satisfying the voyeuristic demands of its readers is not a legitimate interest allowing a tabloid to publish a photo. A photo of Caroline attending the Monte Carlo circus festival would therefore have been acceptable. Making liability dependent on whether publication is a legitimate concern to the public in general[36] was also central to the French case of

---

32 See for English law, e.g., *Rees v Darlington Memorial Hospital NHS Trust* [2003] UKHL 52.
33 Warren and Brandeis 1890.
34 See, e.g., BVerfG 15 December 1999, BVerfGE 101, 361 (*Caroline von Monaco III*).
35 *Caroline von Hannover v Germany*, No. 59320/00, [2004] 40 ECHR 1.
36 See also Restatement (Second) of Torts § 652D (1965).

'Le Grand Secret', the title of a book the former doctor of François Mitterrand published shortly after the former French President died. The book revealed Mitterrand had suffered from prostate cancer from the very first months of his presidency. The French courts banned the publication for violating the dignity of the President and the privacy of his widow and children, but the European Court of Human Rights rightly emphasised that a permanent ban on distribution of the book was disproportionate to the aim pursued and a breach of the right to freedom of expression.[37] The public's right to know outweighed the individual's right to privacy.

The case of an invasion of a personality right is special in one respect. It was previously noted that the deterrent and punitive effect of tort law must be doubted where wrongful behaviour already invokes criminal sanctions. Infringing a personality right usually does not, which could be a reason to allow for high amounts in non-pecuniary damages. This is, in particular, appropriate if the defendant's main aim is shameless commercial exploitation of the claimant's privacy, as with a tabloid aiming to sell many more copies by misusing the celebrity's image and faking interviews. In one of the Caroline of Monaco cases, the German civil court awarded the high amount of 180,000 Deutsche Mark, explicitly arguing this would deter the tabloid from similar behaviour in the future.[38] This is a clear example of how tort law can be used as an instrument to straighten out tabloids or other corporate wrongdoers.

A highly contested question is whether damages for pain and suffering should also be available for the death of a loved one. It may seem self-evident at first sight that such a wrongful death claim should be possible: if anything is a cause for sorrow and grief, it is the death of a spouse, partner or child killed by a tortious act of another person. However, the law considers the claimant in such a case to be only a 'secondary victim' and much can be said against putting a monetary value on loss of love, care, affection and companionship. Is it not precisely the impossibility to compensate this heartbreaking type of grief with money that should stand in the way of compensation? The victim himself can use the non-pecuniary damages as a substitute for what he lost, but awarding €10,000 to a parent who lost a child does not offer any solace. The real reason for bringing this claim therefore probably lies in the wish to punish the tortfeasor or at least to get judicial

---

37 *Plon (Société) v France*, No. 58148/00, [2006] 42 ECHR 36.
38 OLG Hamburg 25 July 1996, NJW 1996, 2870.

recognition: the claimant wants the tortfeasor to realise the effects of his action on third parties. A small amount may then suffice, also because it is not the tortfeasor but the insurer who will likely end up paying. Another argument for not allowing the claim is that it could very well lead to repellent discussions in court wishing to see evidence of the sorrow and of the intensity of the relationship of the claimant to the deceased person. Given the length of court procedures, it may force a widow who is meanwhile into a new relationship to prove she really is still suffering from the passing away of her partner. For all these reasons it is understandable that jurisdictions such as Germany and the Netherlands usually do not allow claims for pain and suffering after the death of a loved one. But a majority of legal systems do, be it oft restricted to a close circle of relatives and limited to a certain amount (e.g., in the case of the UK Fatal Accidents Act 1976 only for the bereaved spouse or parents and for no more than £13,000).

This does not mean no action can be brought against the person responsible for the loss of a loved one. Apart from material damages (such as loss of maintenance) it could happen that, as a result of the accident, the relative is not only angry, sad and frustrated but also develops a psychiatric illness. The best-known example is when a family member suffers from nervous shock (post-traumatic stress disorder, or PTSD) after having witnessed an accident in which a relative dies. In such a case the plaintiff is no longer a secondary victim, but is someone claiming that the defendant committed a tort *directly* against himself. This is fairly easy to prove in French and German law, but not in English law, which requires not only that it was foreseeable for the tortfeasor that the claimant would suffer mental harm through the death of the loved one, but also that he witnessed the accident or its immediate aftermath. This was not a problem when a claimant was called into a hospital after a truck had struck the car of her family. Upon arrival she found one child dead and her husband and two other children seriously injured covered in oil and mud waiting for treatment. She suffered shock and personality change and was able to claim damages: the court still found this the immediate aftermath of the accident.[39] However, no direct confrontation to the accident was established in the Hillsborough football stadium case.[40] The police had been negligent in directing too many spectators to one end of the stadium at an FA cup semi-final. Ninety-five people were crushed to death and many

---

39 *McLoughlin v O'Brian* [1983] AC 410 (HL).
40 *Alcock v Chief Constable of South Yorkshire Police* [1992] 1 AC 310 (HL).

more injured. Claims brought by relatives who saw the disaster live on television, who were in other parts of the ground or were asked to identify their close ones at a mortuary eight hours later, all failed as they had not been close enough. Following this horrendous event from a distance is not the same thing as being within physical sight. The claimants were simply too remote from the crushing, an element also recognised in 'bystander claims' under American law that usually requires the plaintiff to have been in the 'zone of danger'.

3.5   Causation and damages

The nature of tort law, which bases liability on the individual wrong of one person vis-à-vis another, explains why damages only need to be compensated if they are caused by the tortfeasor. Although the use of the term 'caused' seems to imply a simple 'but-for' or *'sine qua non'* test (but for the act, the result would not have happened), this factual causation is never sufficient. If, as a result of a car accident caused by A, B has multiple broken bones, the law has no difficulty in finding a causal link between A's tort and B's injuries. B's losses, as a result of him not being able to work for two months, can also be said to have been caused by A. But what if B, as a result of the accident, gets so depressed that his attempted suicide makes him unable to work for the rest of his life? Is A also liable for this? And what if the accident causes a traffic jam through which C misses his flight to Milan where he was to sign an important contract that would have saved his company from bankruptcy? Is A liable for C's losses or even for the losses suffered by C's employees who are fired as a result of the insolvency? When only applying the 'but-for' test, even A's grandmother can be said to have 'caused' the damage by giving birth to A's father.

This is why, when lawyers require causation, they mean to say that the tortfeasor is only liable for those losses for which the law requires him to be responsible. Causation is a highly normative concept. Although the legal cause coincides in most cases with common sense, legislators, courts and academics have developed painstaking theories on when the link between an event and a loss is legally relevant. These theories go under names such as the remoteness of damage, proximate cause, adequate cause, reasonable attribution or the need for a certain and direct causal connection. No matter which theory is formally applied, their practical application is in fact dependent on a range of different underlying policy reasons. The foreseeability of the damage is one, as is the wish to protect victims in personal injury cases (as opposed to cases in which only economic damage is suffered) and the degree to which the tortfeasor can be blamed for his conduct.

The wish to limit liability in the case of economic damage to what is foreseeable for the defendant can be illustrated by reference to the English case of *The Wagon Mound*.[41] When the tanker 'The Wagon Mound' was refuelled in Sydney harbour, oil spilled by careless employees of the defendant spread to the plaintiff's wharf. The plaintiff was advised that oil on water cannot ignite and therefore continued repair work on a ship. However, two days later molten metal fell in the water and fire broke out anyway, damaging both the ship and the wharf. The court found this damage too remote and reasoned it was not 'of such a kind as the reasonable man should have foreseen'. Pollution of the wharf was foreseeable, not that it would be set alight two days later as a result.

Sacrificing foreseeability on the altar of victim protection, courts are less reluctant to establish a causal link in personal injury cases. If in a slip-and-fall case the victim has more severe injuries than the defendant could anticipate because of an eggshell skull or a weak heart, the latter still needs to make good the extra losses. Similarly, if I run down a professional footballer such as Lionel Messi, I need to pay more lost earnings than if I run down a nurse. In the same vein, I need to pay more in a case where the victim has ME or develops PTSD as a result of the accident. These are mere applications of the maxim that a tortfeasor takes the victim as he finds him.[42] The wrongdoer must make whole the harm he has done to the victim and the simple fact is that not all victims are similar.

There is an extra reason to attribute damage to the tortious act if the tortfeasor did something wrong intentionally or was grossly negligent. There is even more reason for doing so where the defendant is an expert and experienced commercial party. A special case in which not even the 'but-for' test is met, but the defendant is still held liable, concerns the famous DES-cases. DES was a medicine prescribed to pregnant women since the 1940s to prevent them from having a miscarriage. The product was recalled from the market in 1971 when it had become clear that the daughters of DES-users had a higher risk of

---

41 *The Wagon Mound No. 1* [1961] AC 388 (PC).
42 *Smith v Leech Brain Co* [1962] 2 QB 405 (QB).

getting cancer. However, the problem these 'DES-daughters' faced was that, though they were able to prove their damage was caused by the medicine, they could not prove which manufacturer had produced the product their mother had used. Even if their mother was still alive, she naturally had not kept track of the exact provenance of the product she had used. If we assume liability of the pharmaceutical manufacturers is appropriate, the law can deal with this lack of 'but-for' causation in two different ways. One technique was applied by the Supreme Court of California in the case of *Sindell v Abbott Laboratories*.[43] The court found the defendant liable in proportion to its market share: for example, a manufacturer that held 10 per cent of the market for DES was liable for 10 per cent of the claimant's damage. This solution is clearly to the benefit of the manufacturer, who can never be liable for more damage than he caused. However, if the victims want to recover their full damage they have to bring all manufacturers to court, something which is highly unlikely to happen as some of them will no longer exist at the time when the victims became ill. This is why the Dutch *Hoge Raad* choose another solution.[44] It held all manufacturers fully liable for the entire damage but allowed each individual manufacturer to prove the damage was *not* caused by him. As a result the claimant only needs to sue one of the manufacturers, thus shifting the risk that not all manufacturers are still active and solvent away from the victim.

3.6   Looking beyond tort law: alternatives and new interests

It follows from the above that tort law plays an essential role in empowering people to live the lives they wish to live. It protects both the economic interests and the personality of people by allowing them to undertake action against those who infringe upon their autonomy. Tort law thus protects the minimum norms necessary for living together in society, but does not change anything in the existing distribution of economic wealth. Both the homeless and the millionaire are put back into the position they were in before the tort happened. This makes tort law a prime example of corrective justice.

---

43 *Sindell v Abbott Laboratories*, 607 P.2d 924 (Cal. 1980).

44 HR 9 October 1992, NJ 1994, 535 (*DES-daughters*). The House of Lords accepted a similar type of alternative causation in a case of asbestos-related mesothelioma in the case of *Fairchild v Glenhaven Funeral Services Ltd* [2002] 3 WLR 89.

Rhetoric, however, can be deceptive. It is a powerful image that tort law only restores what was wronged, but in reality the field is swamped with policy questions both legislators and courts have to answer and that are necessarily informed by considerations of distributive justice as well. Many such questions were discussed earlier in this chapter and I wish to return to two of them here in a slightly broader context.

The first question is whether the overall aim of tort law is indeed best dealt with by the current rules. It was earlier noted that the central question of tort law is when behaviour is tortious and when it is not. Tort law carves out the specific risk the defendant is liable for because it does not fall within the victim's general risk of living one's life.[45] However, next to tort law, many other, and sometimes better, ways of dealing with the allocation of loss exist. Tort law is certainly not fit to deal with the bulk cases of traffic accidents. If each individual victim of a car accident had to go to court and start a lawsuit this would not only overburden the courts but it would also make compensation dependent on finding a financially healthy defendant. In addition, not every victim will file a claim, leading Atiyah to warn against a 'damages lottery'. Social security and mandatory insurance[46] are both cheaper and quicker means of compensating victims. They relieve both tortfeasor and victim from excruciating efforts to recover their loss and favour an efficient unwinding of the claim by repeat players of insurers and specialised lawyers. In addition, insurance spreads the loss among so many potential tortfeasors (through premiums) that no one really feels it.

The example of mandatory liability insurance for traffic accidents prompts the question of what is the potential for alternative compensation schemes in general. If the aim of the law is not to allow a victim to have his loss made good by the tortfeasor but to receive compensation, this could also be realised by social insurance. New Zealand goes furthest in this respect. Its *Accident Compensation Act* replaces tort law with a mandatory insurance scheme for all personal injuries caused by accident no matter where they happened: on the road, at work, at home, during sports or any other activity. The scheme is not run by private insurers but by a government agency.[47] This exclusion

---

45 Called the '*allgemeines Lebensrisiko*' in German law.

46 Cf. EU-Directive 2009/103 relating to insurance against civil liability in respect of the use of motor vehicles, and the enforcement of the obligation to insure against such liability.

47 See www.acc.co.nz.

of tort law – bringing a claim for personal injury against the tortfeasor is simply not allowed – may sound like a huge step forward in terms of compensating as many people as possible at a reasonable cost, but it is criticised in New Zealand itself from two different sides. Some want to expand insurance and argue that the scheme makes an unjustified discrimination between those who are injured as a result of an accident and those who get ill or suffer from congenital disabilities. Others point at the huge costs and bureaucracy the scheme entails and at its possibly erosive effect on deterrence.

Another means to recompense victims is to create a compensation fund. These are often fed by public money to deal with the consequences of some major catastrophe such as a flooding, a plane crash or a terrorist attack. The September 11th Victim Compensation Fund is a prime example in the United States. Funds can also provide more permanent solutions, as in cases of criminal injuries compensation funds or funds to compensate victims of uninsured drivers. They could also be funded by private money, as in cases of funds for victims of sexual abuse by the Catholic Church. This reiterates that tort law is only one possible solution for dealing with losses. This should prompt policymakers to think through whether they want to allow parties to achieve individualised justice or simply want to adopt an instrument to achieve the regulatory goal of compensation.

The second question concerns the future of fault liability. Despite the rise of alternative no-fault compensation schemes, fault liability remains and is even likely to grow in importance as a result of the increasing wish of people to shift their loss to somebody else. Many a loss considered merely an unhappy incident in the past has become a reason to sue. An unfortunate misstep while playing tennis, a playful push or an injury incurred while helping a friend move house are no longer seen as facts of life, but a reason to pass on the loss to another (preferably solvent) person. This phenomenon, often referred to as the 'blame culture',[48] makes it all the more important to find the boundaries of tort. The above survey of the requirements for the violation of a duty of care, damage and causation shows a continuous struggle to limit liability, and yet allow it to exist when needed. Tort law must try to avoid opening the 'floodgates', the fear of a 'liability in an indeterminate amount for an indeterminate time to an indeterminate class'.[49]

---

48 Fleming 1988.
49 Judge Cardozo in *Ultramares Corporation v Touche*, 174 N.E. 441, 444 (1932).

A very good reason for this is that it would not only put too much pressure on the judiciary but, more importantly, it could also lead to defensive behaviour of potential defendants. The fear of being sued for malpractice could lead doctors to recommend more tests and treatments than is objectively necessary to save a patient. If the police were liable for the omission to arrest someone who turns out a murderer they could be inclined to avoid liability by arresting more people than is legitimate.

The results of this emerging claim culture are clearly visible, be it more in some countries than in others. Litigation against the tobacco industry by claimants that contracted lung cancer as a result of smoking cigarettes is well known. Further questions abound. Should there also be liability of manufacturers of handguns to gunshot victims, of swimming pool manufacturers for death by drowning, and of breweries for alcohol addiction? The impact of such claims is particularly felt if they are brought as a mass claim by large numbers of plaintiffs, as is not uncommon in the United States. In the case *Price v Philip Morris*, for example, 1.4 million claimants filed suit against a tobacco manufacturer for advertising Marlboro Light cigarettes as being less harmful than others. The Illinois appellate court awarded $7.1 billion in compensatory damages and $3 billion in punitive damages.[50] These figures are unheard of elsewhere, but the scope for mass claims by consumers is increasing around the world in order to avoid congestion of the courts and achieve efficiency gains from a collective proceeding.

One possible expansion of tort law lies in the type of interests worth protecting. The history of tort law clearly mirrors changing perceptions of what society finds valuable enough to protect. While the emphasis was first on tangible interests such as the protection of property, life and bodily integrity, a general personality right (including privacy) gradually became protected in the course of the twentieth century. The next step for tort law may be to safeguard interests such as the environment, animal welfare or future generations in general. The protection of these interests traditionally falls within the realm of public law, but the question is whether individuals (or interest groups) must also be given standing to pursue them before the courts. For example, should a claim against the government to reduce carbon emissions by a certain

---

50 *Price v Philip Morris Inc*, 2014 IL App (5th) 130017.

percentage be allowed?[51] This certainly fits the idea of an 'expanding circle' of people to whom we owe obligations.[52] The fundamental concern of tort law is whether these ethical obligations should be turned into legal ones or not.

---

51 Affirmative: District Court of The Hague 24 June 2015, ECLI:NL:RBDHA:2015:7196 (*Urgenda Foundation v State of the Netherlands*).

52 Singer 1981.

4 Property law

4.1 Introduction

A world without property is hard to imagine. Such a world would still have land, houses, cars, books, paintings and companies, but no one would own them. No individual person could exclusively use these assets or transfer them to somebody else. This world remains a fiction: without property rights it is unlikely that people would be willing to purchase, to invest, to invent or to create. The willingness to make a sacrifice is greatly promoted by the benefit to be derived from this.[1] It is therefore no surprise why reinstating private property rights was one of the first tasks the new governments of the former socialist countries set themselves after the fall of the Berlin wall: a well-functioning economy cannot be conceived without protecting property.

The law's involvement with property is about two things: the distribution of property in society and establishing the extent to which people have autonomy in using, disposing and transferring their property. Both these aspects are highly influenced by the nature of property rights: unlike rights arising from contract or tort, property rights can be exerted against the entire world. This mirrors the age-old distinction lawyers make between personal rights and absolute rights: while a personal right can only be exercised against a specific debtor (such as the other contracting party or the tortfeasor) absolute rights are enforceable against everyone (*erga omnes*, as lawyers say in their dog Latin). The owner of a car can keep everyone from using, touching and transferring the car without his consent. It is this far-reaching autonomy that property rights bring to the entitled person that makes it quintessential for these rights to be distributed in a fair way.

This sets the agenda for this chapter. If contracts are about consensual relations and tort law is about accidental interaction, property law can

---

1 Munzer 1990, 15.

be seen as channelling decision-making for scarce resources.[2] The question of how to realise this, and which role the law plays in it, is discussed first (Section 4.2). This frees the way for considering the absoluteness of property rights: how far does the autonomy of the owner in making use of his property actually reach and upon what is this autonomy based? It will be shown that autonomy in property law is a two-edged sword: because property rights can be exercised against the entire world the use, creation and contents of such rights are necessarily limited. This is why the law emphasises the social function of ownership (Section 4.3) and adopts a closed system of property rights (Section 4.4). Three important aspects of the owner's powers are subsequently examined: rights of use (Section 4.5); security rights (Section 4.6) and the right to keep and transfer property (Section 4.7).

However, any systematic treatment of property law must start with the question as to which goods property rights may be vested. Phrasing the question in this way already reveals an important aspect of property law: property lawyers are not interested in land, houses, ships or machinery as such but only in the invisible parallel life of rights *in* these material objects.[3] These could be rights of ownership but also security rights (such as a pledge) or rights of use (such as an easement or servitude). This is well reflected in s. 16 of the English Sale of Goods Act, which speaks of 'property in the goods', while American property lawyers search for a 'title' in the very same manner. Contrary to common parlance, property is therefore not about things but about *rights* to things.[4] The importance of this in actual life is difficult to underestimate: the more rights one can vest in an object, the more wealth one can create. It is very common that quite a few persons have rights in one specific piece of land, ranging from the owner to the mortgagee to the actual user. Economist Hernando de Soto has even argued that the inability of a legal system to accommodate this splitting up of property into various sub-rights is the major source of poverty in the world: '[t]he poor of the world – five-sixths of humanity – have things but they lack the process to represent their property and create capital. They have houses but not titles; lands but not deeds.'[5] This reveals an important function of property law: it can turn 'dead capital' into wealth by creating (valuable) rights.

---

2 Heller 2003, 62.

3 Lawson and Rudden 2002, 5.

4 As already noted by Bentham 1789, ch. XVI, § 26.

5 De Soto 2000, 6–7.

Property rights can exist in a great variety of objects, ranging from tangible goods such as land and computers, to intangible objects such as claims against others, radio spectra and inventions, literary texts, music and other intellectual and artistic products. In fact, most of today's wealth is not tangible: entitlements arising from government bonds, shares, intellectual property rights and bank accounts probably represent a much higher value than rights in land or any other touchable goods. In a celebrated article on 'the new property', the American author Charles Reich goes even further and incorporates in his definition of property any entitlements to wealth outside of traditional ownership of land and objects, such as drivers' licences, insurance, membership of the bar, franchises and welfare assistance to the poor.[6] Looked at in this way, the fact that something is classified as property means it is believed to have a market value. Property rights in land only came about when people started to plough it. And it took until the eighteenth century before the Indians felt a need to develop property rights in animals as only at this point in time a demand for fur arose. But this does not end controversy at the fringes. The mere fact that objects have a high value does not necessarily make them susceptible for property, as the examples of kidneys, embryos and children put up for adoption show. There is more than a grain of truth in the saying that the world's most valuable things are priceless.

It was already observed in Chapter 2 that the law's affinity with generalisation does not always have an easy fit with differences in the significance of law in real life. Property law is not any different. Ownership enables people not only to have clothes on their back, food in their stomach and a roof over their head but also to obtain many other things beyond their immediate wants. The very same legal concept of mortgage is used both by the house owner who gets evicted from his flat if he no longer pays the monthly interest, and the large company obtaining a loan to finance its latest investment. In the same vein, there is a world of difference between owning a piece of land, a pen or a patent. Such a differentiation of property rights according to the object on which they rest was a key feature of the former socialist countries. For example, the 1977 Constitution of the Union of Soviet Socialist Republics (USSR) distinguished between state property (extending to the means of production, land, industry and natural resources), collective property (in particular of farms) and personal property.[7] The

---

6 Reich 1964.
7 Arts. 10–13.

latter could only rest on consumption, savings from labour and household goods (such as clothing, a copy of the collected works of Karl Marx and possibly a car if one was lucky enough to be allowed to buy one). Although this distinction can no longer be found in existing legislation, it still plays a role in the background in most legal systems. Thus, even in insolvency an individual can keep his bed, clothes, fridge and furniture. In addition, people's small savings enjoy a high protection against failing banks. Evicting the inhabitant from residential property is generally also more difficult than evicting a business from their offices. Finally, it will be shown that land has always had a special status; the state can always expropriate it in the public interest if a fair compensation is paid.

4.2   Distribution and regulation of property

The question of what should be the proper distribution of property, wealth and income is one of the most fundamental issues a society can face. The richest 1 per cent of today's world population possesses half of its wealth and is likely to become even richer.[8] Whether such inequality is justified depends entirely on which view of justice one adopts. Libertarians such as Robert Nozick do not consider this too much of a problem. They argue that any given distribution of wealth is just as long as it is historically justified. This is the case if it is the result of, first, possession of un-owned land (until the Industrial Revolution land was by far the most valuable asset people could have) and, subsequently, transactions freely entered into by citizens to transfer their land to others.[9] Egalitarians, however, hold that resources must be distributed more equally. For example, in John Rawls' account of justice as fairness, the political and personal liberty of everyone in society can only be guaranteed if wealth is not distributed too unevenly. Rawls' so-called 'property-owning democracy' must therefore ensure a widespread ownership of not only human capital (such as education) but also of assets. Only this will allow equal opportunities for everyone.[10] This does not mean that inequality in income or wealth is unacceptable but it must bring benefit to individuals with the least income. Progressive taxation is commonly agreed upon as the best way to realise this.

---

8 As emphasised by Piketty 2013.
9 Nozick 1974.
10 Rawls 2001, 139.

This is not just a philosophical discussion. Some of the world's most important political events were at least partly caused by dissatisfaction with existing differences in the spread of wealth. This is not only true for the French Revolution of 1789 and the Russian one of 1917 but also for the fall of the Berlin Wall in 1989 and the end of Apartheid in South Africa. Freedom and equality of people are difficult to achieve if people do not have the real capability to acquire property. The Universal Declaration of Human Rights of 1948 reflects this by holding that 'everyone has the right to own property', thus refuting a long list of reputed authors who see value in keeping all property common. They range from Socrates, arguing that property, like wives and children, is best shared among the men in order to avoid conflict and buy time to be spent on matters of the state,[11] to Jean-Jacques Rousseau, who saw private property as it emerged after man left the state of nature as the source of all evil, inequality, misery and horror.[12] The practical value of these Utopian ideas has ended with the demise of the Communist experiment in the second half of the twentieth century but they do contain a stark reminder of the need to strike a balance between the individual powers of owners and the community interest. All societies are in need of a 'proprietary constitution'[13] regulating the access to, and use of, scarce goods.

At a more concrete level, this need for the regulation of scarce resources is best illustrated by reference to the famed Tragedy of the Commons as identified by the American ecologist Garrett Hardin. Hardin warns about the risk of overuse if too many people have access to a resource. If a pasture is open to all, each herdsman will keep as many cattle as possible on the commons. This works well as long as the number of mouths to be fed remains the same, but with a growing population each rancher has an incentive to add more animals to the meadow. This leads to overgrazing, but as long as each individual herder will still make more money by adding another cow he is unlikely to abstain from this. In the end the pasture becomes useless and all will starve. Hardin comments: '[e]ach man is locked into a system that compels him to increase his herd without limit – in a world that is limited . . . Freedom in a commons brings ruin to all'.[14] This is a powerful meta-phor that can be applied to any case where a user gets the entire benefit

---

11 As described in Plato's *Republic*, Book V, 457C, 462B.
12 Rousseau 1755.
13 Mattei 2000, 30.
14 Hardin 1968, 1244.

of the use but is still able to share the costs with all other users. Filthy public toilets provide another case in point. The only way to avoid this is to regulate the access to common goods. Having said this, it would be a mistake to limit access to only a few people. This could, in turn, result in a tragedy of 'anticommons':[15] if those with exclusive access to a resource veto each other's use, under-exploitation is the likely result. A sad example of this is the phenomenon of abandoned houses in the South of Europe, where each individual co-heir has an incentive to block the competence of the other co-heirs in selling the property.[16] The law must find a middle ground so as to avoid both tragedies.

It is not difficult to create such a proprietary constitution at the national level, where legislators and courts have invariably come up with detailed rules on the distribution and use of shared resources. For example, many (local) governments provide incentives to tenants in public housing to buy the house they live in. This is at least partly inspired by the fact that public housing is often badly maintained by the tenants and it is assumed owners would take better care. But also the access to water, healthcare, forests, museums and many other collective goods is usually heavily regulated. This type of regulation is much more difficult to realise when a political framework is lacking. Unfortunately, this is exactly the case when it comes to some of the major problems the world is facing today. One example is the depletion of fish in the ocean, where each individual fisherman has no incentive to restrain himself in catching as many fish as possible. Another example is global climate change. The atmosphere is a perfect example of a commons as each individual has a benefit to keep driving her car and lighting her house while sharing the costs of these harmful activities with the entire world. No individual who abstains from doing this will be able substantially to affect the total emission of greenhouse gases. Both overfishing and global warming are therefore in need of a global proprietary constitution. This need not come about by way of an international treaty but could also be built by national courts enforcing common norms for a sustainable world.

---

15 Heller 1998.
16 The example is provided by Mattei 2000, 2.

4.3   Autonomy in using ownership: between liberty and social function

Legislators excel in making rhetorical statements about property. True to the post-revolutionary spirit (the 1789 Declaration of the Rights of Man and of the Citizen had already declared property as a right 'sacred and inviolable'), Art. 544 of the French Civil Code describes ownership as 'the right to enjoy and dispose of things in the most complete manner'. This absolute right to exclude all others from doing anything with one's property, and to use it in whatever way desired, can also be found in other codes but was perhaps best formulated by the most famous English lawyer of all time. In his Commentaries on the Laws of England, William Blackstone qualified property as 'that sole and despotic dominion which one man claims and exercises over the external things of the world, in total exclusion of the right of any other individual in the universe'.[17] There is no better illustration of this than the sign still deployed by quite a few landowners in the American countryside and reading: 'trespassers will be shot'.

As many other things in law, this emphasis on the absolute character of property rights can only be understood from history. It is a product of natural law thinking that everyone must have a free sphere in which one can do, and not do, as one pleases. Protection of private property is in this sense the protection of individual freedom against intervention by others.[18] The real revolution this type of thinking brought about was that the right holder was no longer under any duty to *do* something. This was different in times of feudalism, when the use of land was invariably tied to all kinds of personal obligations. The farmer not only had to endure that the nobleman damaged the crops while hunting on his land but also had to give part of the harvest (or what was left of it) to his lord, act as a soldier in his army or even marry the person the lord designated. The law radically broke with these practices after the French Revolution. This explains why still today property law is highly reluctant to put a positive burden on the owner of land without his consent – except for the duty to pay taxes. *Noblesse oblige*, ownership does not.

While the rhetoric of property as an absolute right thus still applies to the owner's right *not* to do anything, this is much less the case for the

---

17 Blackstone 1765–69, Book 2, 1.

18 For a modern defense of property as liberty, see Waldron 1988, 329: 'People need private property for the development and exercise of their liberty'.

owner's right to *do* with the object as he pleases. In theory, the owner of a plot of land has the power to fence the land, to use the subsoil, to use the water and to plant and build on it, but in reality this power is heavily restricted in at least three different ways.

First and foremost, administrative regulations often limit the owner in what he can do with his property. Building regulations, environmental requirements, rules on zoning and on tenancy law all heavily restrict the freedom of the owner of an immovable. It is far from it that the owner could decide all by himself to destroy a house on his land or even to cut down a tree without prior permission of the local authority. The use of movable objects is usually less regulated. True, the driver of a car is bound to meet strict requirements (have a driver's licence, obtain mandatory insurance, etc.) and the owner of a dog is not allowed to injure it, but these are not specifically duties falling upon the owner but on anyone wishing to drive a car or crossing the animal's path.

Second, as is always the case in the law, a right ends where another man's right begins. This is well reflected in Art. 5:1(2) of the Dutch Civil Code that states: '[t]o the exclusion of all others, the owner is free to use the object provided that this use does not violate the rights of others . . .'. The owner is obviously not allowed to make use of his property if his only aim is to intentionally harm others. He may, for example, not erect a dummy chimney on his roof to deprive the neighbour of daylight or build a water tower without any connection to the water conduits so as to irritate a nearby landowner.[19] But property rights are not only curtailed in these obvious cases of abuse of rights. Their use must also be proportionate. I am surely allowed to use a device to scare away wild animals from my farm in Africa. But this is different if I use an electronic scarecrow that makes a loud noise every ten minutes preventing my neighbours from sleeping. And if the nearby garbage dump, even when operating with a licence, attracts crows and rooks eating the fruit and vegetables in my orchard, I can oblige the dump to take measures to avoid this in the future. I could even be prevented from destroying an object that I own: the maker of a painting or the architect of a celebrated building may claim I am abusing my property right if I demolish their artistic work.

Third, the use of property rights must not go against the community

---

19 Respectively, Cour d'appel de Colmar 2 May 1855, D. 1856, 2, 9 and Hoge Raad 13 March 1936, NJ 1936, 415.

interest. When Portalis presented his draft of the civil code to the French legislator, he wrote that 'true freedom consists of a wise balance of rights and individual powers and the common good'.[20] A modern formulation can be found in Art. 14(2) of the German Constitution: '[p]roperty entails obligations. Its use shall also serve the public good'. This idea of property not only being a right but also having a social function is of all times, but it regained prominence again as a reaction to the liberal view of property prevailing in the nineteenth century. The French Civil Code of 1804 is not without reason often referred to as the 'code of the owner'. The Code lacks a general part on private law, on the law of obligations and on the law of succession but instead places all three topics in the book on 'ways to acquire property'. It does not, therefore, come as a surprise that in particular in France the counter-reaction to this dominance of ownership was highly influential. The pendulum always swings back, as evidenced in the emphasis Léon Duguit (1859–1928) put on the owner being inherently limited in his property rights.[21]

Now, the true question is, of course, when exactly the use of private property goes against the common good. One case is readily accepted everywhere: expropriation in the public interest. The state or another government entity is allowed to take private property to build roads, install pipes, erect buildings or for any other public purpose, provided a just compensation is paid. Expropriation is even regarded as such an invasion of individual rights that many jurisdictions provide for it in their constitutions.[22] This brings the protection of property against the state ultimately under the scrutiny of the constitutional court and, in the case of Europe, within the competence of the European Court of Human Rights. An example comes from the rich American case law on expropriation (or power of eminent domain, as it is called there after the Latin term coined by Grotius[23]). In *Lucas v South Carolina Coastal Council*,[24] property developer David Lucas purchased some seaside real estate on the Isle of Palms with a view to develop it as residential property and then resell it. Shortly thereafter South Carolina enacted a new statute to preserve beaches in the area, making it impossible to build anything and thus making Lucas' investment worthless. The US

---

20 Portalis 1803, 77; for a contemporary restatement, Alexander 2009.
21 Duguit 1920, 21.
22 Ackerman 1977.
23 Grotius 1625, Book I, ch. III, s. VI, 2.
24 505 US 1003 (1992).

Supreme Court found this to be a violation of the Fifth Amendment to the US Constitution (protecting private property) and South Carolina was forced to repay Lucas the amount he had bought the property for. In many ways this far-going power of the state confirms the view that no private person is allowed to have the supreme right to the land. This is a view English law in particular is happy to entertain by adopting the fiction that the Crown is the owner of all the land. But in fact any jurisdiction accepting expropriation adheres to the idea of all property being held subject to the state; it is what an Australian court rightly called the 'proprietary aspect of sovereignty'.[25]

The more fascinating question is whether the common good must be given an even broader meaning. For example, should each owner have a social obligation to use his assets in conformity with the community interest? This could mean that the owner can use, but not 'use up', the resource. This is not the position of the current law but pleas have been made that it should be. One could even go one step further and argue that certain commodities such as provision of water, transportation, waste disposal and energy should be neither private nor public, but should instead be designed as a commons as a service to the community and as a guarantee for future generations. The goal is then not to sell a maximum volume of water or energy in order to make a profit, but to save as much of these resources as possible in order to make the legal system more in tune with nature and the community.[26]

4.4   Property rights: standardisation and publicity

Property law is not only about ownership. Far more important than the owner's ability to use and transfer the object in which he has a right is his power to create new rights. If the miracle of multiplication ever occurs, it is in the law of property. For example, the owner can decide to put a mortgage on his house, burden it with a right of way in favour of the neighbour and allow his children to live in the house by giving them the right of usufruct. In turn, each of these individual right holders is again able not only to transfer their right to somebody else but also to create a property right on their 'sub-right': many an usufruct on an immovable is burdened with a security right. One popular way to depict this is to look at property as an aggregate of separate powers (or

25 *Minister of State for the Army v Dalziel* [1944] 68 CLR 261 at 284.
26 Capra and Mattei 2015, 165.

a bundle of rights[27]). The full owner is allowed to exercise all powers, but only in so far as he or his predecessors did not give them away. This may lead to the owner having practically no powers left in his bundle, as in the above example of the house owner. But even then it is still useful to distinguish a separate right of ownership, not only because this right can still be transferred to somebody else, but also because the mortgage and the usufruct (and possibly the right of way) will come to an end after a set time period, after which the owner automatically reassembles the entire bundle of sticks.

The various proprietary sub-rights have the same characteristics as the right to ownership itself: they give the right holder an exclusive power to be exercised against the entire world. The mortgagee and usufructuary can keep everyone from interfering with their rights, even if the object in which the right rests falls into the hands of another person. If the owner sells his house to somebody else, this so-called *droit de suite* ensures that the new owner must still respect the holders of 'real rights' (*rights in rem*) with respect to the house. While this is the logical result of framing one's right as a real right, and not as a mere contractual one, it does present a puzzle for the lawmaker: if these real rights have such a far-going effect, how can third parties recognise these rights were established on the object to the benefit of a specific party? This is not a problem in the case of ownership because one can assume an owner exists for virtually every valuable object around, whether movable or immovable. However, when seeing that very same object it is impossible to discern whether any *other* real right than ownership rests on it. The strategy of the lawmaker in this respect is twofold: it limits the autonomy of parties by standardising the types of real rights that can be established *and* it requires some form of publicity before the real right can have effect against third parties.

The first strategy is to standardise the types of real rights being up for choice. Parties are not allowed to create their own type of real right, but must choose from a set menu provided by the lawmaker. As a result of this so-called *numerus clausus* or *Typenzwang*, only a limited number of property entitlements are accepted. Famous is the 'pentarchy' developed in 1639 by law student Heinrich Hahn, who claimed only five real rights are allowed to exist; most modern jurisdictions may accept a few more but certainly no more than eight. The reason for this far-going inroad on party autonomy is simple enough: if two parties were able

---

27 Hohfeld 1946.

to create a new real right among themselves, this would gravely affect the freedom of third parties who would be bound to respect a right they never heard of before. In addition, if the right holder transferring his right to somebody else were to explain extensively what his right exactly consists of (with the risk of mistakes) this would undermine the certainty needed in economic life and induce unnecessary litigation. It is much easier simply to point out that one has a servitude, mortgage or usufruct of which everyone will know, or can look up, what it entails. If burdens on land or movables are not clear enough this will limit their transferability.[28] In other words: the *erga omnes* effect of property rights comes at the price of limiting party autonomy in both the creation of new rights and in determining the contents of existing rights.

However, mere standardisation is not enough to justify that real rights have effect towards third parties. The law may limit the available real rights by providing a fixed catalogue, but this says nothing about whether these rights were also established on *this* specific object to the benefit of *this* specific person. This is why lawmakers complement it with a second strategy: they require some form of publicity allowing people to verify whether the object is in fact encumbered with a real right or not. Many jurisdictions have a public land register containing information about ownership, mortgages, servitudes and easements. Unfortunately, this does not mean that one can find all rights on a parcel of land by just lifting a file at some public office or by clicking a button on a website. Land registries differ significantly from one jurisdiction to another. Some (as in France) do not offer absolute certainty about who has which right and still require a, sometimes extensive, search by a civil notary. Others (as in Germany and England) offer more certainty, at least in so far as the land is registered at all. Most certainty is offered by the Torrens system, named after the member of the Australian Parliament who proposed it. This system, not only used in Australia but also in Israel and parts of Canada, provides title by registration: only a change of the record in the register can lead to a transfer of ownership. Easements and other real rights must also be registered in order to provide 'indefeasibility' of the right against third parties.

The requirement of publicity is more difficult to realise outside of immovable objects. It would be highly impracticable if one were to register the transfer of ownership of a bike, a book or a pen, let alone

---

28 Rudden 1987; Heller 2003, 70 ff; Akkermans 2008.

the creation of a real right on these objects. The only movable goods for which registries exist are goods of high value such as large ships and aircraft. For other valuable movables, it would in theory be possible simply to brand or label the object, but this is not the solution the law chooses. Instead it makes use of a straightforward presumption: the possessor is regarded as the owner. Anyone who has physical control over an object signals to the outside world that he has the strongest right. Thus, s. 5(1) of the English Theft Act 1968 describes property as belonging to 'any person having possession or control of it', while Art. 2276 of the French Civil Code offers the more succinct formulation: '[p]ossession equals title'.[29] The great benefit of this approach is that the purchaser of the good need not engage in a long and costly search for the owner: he can rely on the person having the factual control to provide him with the title.[30] Even if the possessor was not the actual owner (from whom the good was stolen), the purchaser may still obtain ownership when acting in good faith (see Section 4.7). This rough signal possession sends to the outside world also works well when establishing the age-old security right of a possessory pledge, but it offers no solution for establishing other real rights in movables, let alone in intangible objects such as claims and inventions. The question of how one is to establish a security right in those cases will be discussed in Section 4.6.

4.5   Rights of use

So far little has been said about the contents of real rights although this is evidently an essential issue: limiting the number of real rights only makes sense if their contents are fixed. However, this does not mean parties, when making their choice from the given menu, lack all freedom in agreeing upon the contents of the right. In fact, parties have quite some leeway in designing their proprietary interest in the way they prefer. What all real rights have in common, though, is the law recognising that a mere contractual relationship is not enough to suit the needs of society and economy. For each real right there is a clear need to have the right run with the land or the object, thus making it enforceable against everyone.

This is probably most apparent in the case of rights of use. These pro-

---

29 '*En fait de meubles, la possession vaut titre*'.
30 Cf. Mattei 2000, 110.

vide the right holder with the competence to use or enjoy an object. For example, house owner A may wish to make use of a road on B's property in order to reach his house. He could make a simple contract with B, allowing him to use the road whenever he wishes, but this solution would only allow A to use the road as long as B remains the owner of the land. A's right would end the moment B sells his land to somebody else. The better solution is therefore to establish a real right burdening B's property to the benefit of A's property. Unlike a contractual right, such a *servitude* (the term used in civil law and in the American Restatement (Third) on Property), *easement* or *covenant* (the terms used in English law) survives if B sells his burdened land to a third party. In addition, if A decides to sell his so-called dominant land, the right passes automatically to the new (or any other successive) owners. Put differently: this real right of use runs with the land, independent of the person who owns it.

Servitudes are a highly effective way to ensure that the parties' agreement lasts beyond their own involvement. Although they can only oblige a party to endure, and not to actively do something, they can still be used for the creation of a great variety of rights, including rights of way, to park a car, to light, to allow the flow of water or to preserve trees. Public authorities involved in land development frequently use servitudes as well. For example, if a municipality wishes to sell a plot of land to a project developer it could, by way of a covenant, restrict the use of the land to residential use only. This ensures that the new owners, who will buy their property from the developer, and any of their successors, will respect the area's residential value and refrain from opening up shops on the premises. Some jurisdictions even allow a non-compete clause to be put into the form of a servitude: the chef selling the property adjacent to his restaurant could then establish the servitude that anyone owning that property will not be allowed to open another restaurant in it.

Servitudes present a relatively light burden on the servient land. A right of way, for example, usually only results in the owner having to share a competence, not in abandoning his own right to walk on the land. But sometimes parties are in need of farther-reaching rights and the law facilitates this desire. The civil law right of *usufruct* is one such right. It allows a party to exclusively use and enjoy a good belonging to somebody else. The corny example is the right to collect the yearly harvest or the produce of animals (such as milk and eggs). Even though the right holder does not own the land, the cows or the poultry, he does become the owner of their produce. More relevant in today's society is a usufruct allowing the use of a car or allowing someone to collect the rent. In real life usufruct is frequently used for an even more important purpose: arranging for the disposal of one's assets after death. Giving one's surviving partner a right of usufruct on the house allows him or her to continue to live there and enforce the right against the heirs (typically the children) who have become the new owners. This explains why most rights of usufruct are created by way of a will and typically end upon the death of the usufructuary.

Another far-reaching right of use is the right civil lawyers refer to as *emphyteusis* and that bears great resemblance with the *leasehold* in common law. This right follows from the societal need to allow people to exercise virtually all rights in the bundle of property, be it under the conditions set by the owner. Emphyteusis (and leasehold in English law) thus gives the right holder the power to hold and to use the immovable, to build upon it, to transfer his right to somebody else and to burden it with another real right (such as a mortgage or even a sub-emphyteusis). However, the owner usually sets the conditions under which the long-lessee is allowed to exercise these powers. These conditions are not only likely to oblige the long-lessee to pay an annual sum to the owner but will also limit the right holder in his power to transfer the property to just anyone else. In the Netherlands, for example, large towns like Amsterdam and Rotterdam have long been keen users of emphyteusis as an instrument to prevent speculation on the real estate market and to have the entire community profit from the increased value of land. These municipalities thus greatly influence the use of the land, including who is to live in the newly built houses (e.g. only those with a low income) or even the employment conditions of the employees who will work in the industry established on the premises. It fits the idea of a prevailing community interest that the emphyteusis is only established for a set period of, for example, 99 years after which the owner can again decide what it wants to do with the property.

An important question is whether the owner of an immovable is also allowed, not only to create a real right, but also to split off part of his *ownership* itself for the benefit of somebody else. Would it, for example, be possible to separate the ownership of a house from the ground on which it is built, or of a tree from the land on which it stands? In principle, the law finds this difficult to accept. It prefers to apply the principle of *superficies solo cedit*, meaning everything built on, or part of, the soil forms part of the property. This rule is, again, inspired by the wish not to confront third parties with unexpected property rights: anyone wishing to purchase a plot of land or a building must be able to rely on the outward appearance that he is obtaining everything apparently part of the immovable. This limits search costs, as one need not find out who owns what. However, this is not a real incentive for a builder, farmer or anyone else who wishes to invest in or on the soil of another. A football club aiming to build a clubhouse and an electricity company wishing to put cables in the ground will refrain from doing so if the return on their investment is as short-lived as the ownership of the land of the current owner.

This is why the lawmaker allows people to make use of the real right of *superficies*. This is the right to have ownership in a building, or plants in or on an immovable object, belonging to somebody else. The lesson to be drawn here is that, in law, nothing is by its very nature indivisible. In the parallel world of rights, any object can be subdivided into separate entities as long as it is possible to make this known to the outside world. This makes it difficult to have ownership in separate parts of movables, but relatively easy for immovables, as a public register is available to register the right. But here, too, limits are set by reasonable expectations of people: one need not reckon with separate ownership of a room in a building if there is no separate entry. And if there is one, the appropriate way to design the right is a *leasehold* or *apartment* ownership (or *condominium*), the latter providing the resident with a share in the building and an exclusive right to use a certain part of it. But, as always, the interesting discussion takes place at the fringes of the law. For example, would it also be possible to have separate ownership of street art, like the graffiti painting Banksy put on a brick wall? The fact that the painting may be worth more than the stones on which it appears could be an argument pointing in this direction.

This brief survey shows that rights of use are particularly relevant for immovable property. This is no surprise: land and buildings are bound to last for a long time, generally represent a high value and by their very nature remain at one location, allowing for an easy check in the public register. This special position of immovable property comes out clearly in English law, which does not apply one unitary property law regardless of the object but has separate rules for land and personal (i.e. movable) property. English land law still reflects the feudal idea that ownership must rest with the King and that all others can only have a right derived from this. This so-called *estate* can be eternal (a *freehold* or *fee simple*) or for a limited period of time (a *leasehold*), even though 'limited' must sometimes be taken with a grain of salt: although 99 years is a usual period, the lease can last for 999 or even 3,000 years.

It goes without saying that parties are not in need of real rights in order to use a house or an office. They are also able to rent it for a limited period of time and simply become the tenants of the immovable property. Even though this tenancy agreement provides the parties with only personal claims against each other, many national legislators provide the tenant with a protection coming close to having a real right. They apply the rule 'sale does not break lease': if the landlord decides to sell the property, the new owner is usually bound to the lease (as well as entitled to the rent). The terms of the agreement remain intact and only the identity of the landlord changes. This turns tenancy into a 'half real right'; it would be a full one if not only the tenant could enforce his rights against the new landlord, but also a new tenant could do so against the existing landlord. This, however, is not the case: the tenant himself cannot transfer his right to live in the house to another person without the landlord's consent.

So far no attention has been paid to a specific right of use that is not vested in a tangible good (and is therefore not a 'real right') but in a product of the mind. Intellectual property rights provide their holder with the exclusive right to control the use and distribution of protected objects (such as an invention, novel, song, copyrighted work or trademark) to the public.[31] What intellectual property rights share with other property rights is that they can be enforced against everyone, but they also differ in some important respects from rights in tangible property. These differences, however, are more of a gradual than of a principled nature.

The most distinctive trait of intellectual property rights is that their scope of application is always limited to a specific territory and time period. For example, a patent right can usually only be enforced within one country for a limited time. This makes intellectual property rights ideal to be put to use: if not one person has an exclusive patent but bespoke territorial licences exist for Germany, China and every other country in the world, this is a great instrument to create wealth. An additional benefit is that, unlike tangible goods, intellectual property rights are likely to abound. Available land is finite; the human imagina-

---

31 Gordon 2003.

tion is not.

This fragmentation, not to say balkanisation, of intellectual property rights underlines the power of the right holder. The underlying rationale is that inventors, artists and authors must be able to recover the costs of creation and make a profit out of their creativity. This prevents anyone else from putting the invention or book to commercial use. Although this seems the most natural thing in the world, the idea that one should obtain a 'property' right in one's own creation only received footing in the work of John Locke (1632–1704). Locke reasoned that, as man has power over his body, what he makes with his own labour must belong to him.[32] Although Locke thought of catching fish and picking apples from a wild tree, his utilitarian reasoning applies wonderfully well to products of the mind. Rewards stimulate people to do creative work and thus advance the causes of technique, medicine and culture. But this incentive must not always prevail: another element of the fragmented nature of intellectual property rights is that they are also limited in time in the interest of the general public. For example, patents often last only for 20 years and copyrights for 70 years. This allows inventions and artistic products to be exploited by everyone after their creator has been able to recoup the costs and make a profit. The public interest could even prescribe an obligation actually to use the right to avoid under-exploitation, as in the case of a compulsory licence to produce a medicine vital to public health. In this sense IP law could provide a source of inspiration for a property law more geared towards the interests of the community.

4.6   Property rights as security

Property rights are not only about the right to use and enjoy an object. They also fulfil a vital role in economic life as a means to ensure compliance with an obligation.[33] One of the biggest worries of economic actors is that their counterpart will not pay the price or deliver the goods because of insolvency. This will, of course, allow the creditor to go to court and execute the assets of the debtor but in doing so he has to compete with all other creditors. The principle of *paritas creditorum*, meaning that all available assets must be equally distributed among the creditors, will not make an individual creditor very happy.

---

32   Locke 1689, § II.32.
33   Sagaert, in Van Erp and Akkermans 2012, 425 ff.

He must have a better right than all the others, also because the tax authorities are likely to take the first heap out of the debtor's assets. This is why each major creditor will want to secure performance by way of a security interest giving him priority over everyone else.

A claim can be secured in two different ways: by a person and by an object. Personal surety comes in the form of a guarantee by a person other than the direct debtor who agrees to be liable for the debt. This is a dangerous instrument: it is easy to promise without realising that one may actually have to pay. Even if a personal surety must be made in writing in order to be valid, as many jurisdictions hold in order to make the surety realise what he is getting into, case law provides a steady stream of tragic stories about ruined sureties. An additional risk of personal security for the creditor is that in today's world persons tend to be highly mobile and may disappear. This explains why creditors usually prefer to have security on an object. These real security rights are part of the catalogue of real rights and therefore come with the advantage of being enforceable against everyone.

One security right highly popular among both moneylenders and house owners is the *hypothec* (usually named a mortgage in the English-speaking world but in English law itself technically a charge on land).[34] As land and buildings are unlikely to disappear and cannot be stolen, a hypothec provides an effective form of security for the lender, while from the viewpoint of the borrower it is an excellent way to raise capital. It has the additional advantage that it needs to be registered in the public register in order to have effect against the outside world. If the debtor defaults in paying back the loan or the monthly interest, the lender is allowed to seize the object and sell it. Otherwise, the hypothec automatically comes to an end when the debt is paid off.[35]

More problematic is the creation of a security right on a movable. This traditionally takes the form of a *possessory pledge*, requiring the borrower to hand over the collateral to the lender. This is exactly what happens if an individual brings her vintage car or jewellery to a pawn-broker in order to obtain a loan. Despite the fact that such a pledge can now in many cases also be arranged over the Internet,[36] it continues to

---

34 Under the Land Registration Act 2002.

35 Varieties do exist; the non-accessory German *Grundschuld* is a type of mortgage independent of the lender's claim.

36 See, e.g., www.pawngo.com and www.valendo.de.

suffer from one major problem: the need to hand over the object. The very good reason why the law insists on this requirement is – again – the need to inform third parties about the encumbrance of the asset. It was noted that this warning lies in registration in the case of an immovable. In the case of a movable object, it lies in the de-possession of the owner: if the borrower must abandon the object, it gives the signal to potential lenders that any goods remaining with the debtor are not yet encumbered. However, this rule is not practical at all in commercial life because it gravely limits the assets being able to serve as collateral. The business borrowing money to buy an inventory would not be able to earn the money necessary to pay back the debt if it were to hand over the newly acquired goods to the bank. Legal academics like to pose this as a choice for the lawmaker either to expand security to support lending, and through this economic development, or to keep the system closed in order to protect future lenders.[37] However, the vexed history of non-possessory security shows that legal practice finds its own ways, downplaying the requirement of publicity, and allowing economic intercourse to go full speed ahead.

This is most obvious with a type of security that does not need the intervention of the lawmaker at all and is cheap and easy to realise. This is to use ownership itself as a security instrument. In many a case the seller is willing to deliver goods provided he remains on as their owner until the price is fully paid. Such a retention of title is perfectly valid and in many jurisdictions it will also have effect towards third parties, even though the latter are unable to tell that the goods they see at the buyer's place do not belong to him. This reservation of ownership is highly popular in commercial relationships, but is also widely used by retailers in the form of 'hire-purchase' contracts when selling cars, electronics and other expensive products to consumers. The latter then obtain the right to use the object, but only become the owner when all monthly instalments are paid. In case of the debtor's insolvency the seller is simply able to claim the goods as his property.

Another type of non-possessory security is the *fiducia cum creditore* or transfer of ownership for security purposes. It already existed in Roman times and entails that the moneylender becomes the owner of the goods, but leaves these with the debtor who must rely on the lender's promise to transfer back the ownership when the loan is paid off. This is obviously not an ideally designed right. The creditor not only obtains much

37 Helsen 2015, 962.

more power than he needs – the full property and not simply a security right – but the right is also not apparent to third parties: a potential lender is not able to tell whether the ownership of the painting on the wall or the car in the garage was transferred to somebody else. He will be entirely dependent on what his counterpart tells him about his existing obligations. This is why some national legislators have at times been critical about the rise – since the late nineteenth century – of ownership for security purposes. The Dutch legislator has even formally prohibited it and has created the new institution of a non-possessory pledge with a faint form of publicity, while in other jurisdictions (such as Germany) there are continuous pleas to create a public register for non-possessory security rights. This is also the solution chosen in the United States. Article 9 of the UCC adopts a functional approach towards secured transactions: any right, no matter how it is called, that qualifies as a security interest will only be perfected (meaning it has an *erga omnes* effect) after registration with a filing office. The great advantage of this approach is that it does not matter whether the right is a retention of title, a fiduciary transfer or a pledge: whoever files the collateral first, will be the first in right. A proposed model law for the European Union has suggested also adopting this approach and establishing an online European register of proprietary security.[38]

Registration will clearly only have the desired effect of protecting third parties if the encumbered assets are sufficiently defined. Ideally, it is clear at every moment in time which individualised objects qualify as collateral. However, this ideal is difficult to attain if the debtor's inventory or the claims he has on his own debtors are encumbered, as both types of assets are likely to change by the day. The same is true if the security right rests on shares or intellectual property rights. At the same time, lenders often feel the need to obtain a security right that is as general as possible, covering everything that the debtor owns on any given day including claims on others. English law, perhaps driven by an unrivalled desire to accommodate the needs of business parties, facilitates this by accepting a so-called *floating charge*. This is a registered general security right on changing assets of a commercial party, including land, movables and claims. It crystallises in the form of a fixed charge at the moment the debtor defaults. Other jurisdictions adopt likeminded solutions.

---

38 Art. IX.-3:102 DCFR.

4.7   The right to keep and transfer property

A final aspect of the owner's power is his right either to keep the (property rights in the) goods or to transfer these to somebody else. Textbooks on property law usually do not pay much attention to the first aspect. Lawyers take the existing distribution of property rights as a given and are only interested in the *voluntary* transfer of these rights. They have Montesquieu on their side where he wrote that the public good always consists in everyone keeping the property given to him by private law.[39] This means that property law is not likely to go farther back than the last transaction and has difficulty in accommodating claims based on alleged injustices of the past. A painful example of this blind spot is the occupation of land held by native tribes. When Western settlers took the land of the original population in the American West and Australia, they relied on the myth of an empty land on which they acquired a first title by cultivating or fencing it. This is what society found normal at the time; or as Rousseau put it: '*Le premier qui, ayant enclos un terrain, s'avisa de dire, Ceci est à moi, et trouva des gens assez simples pour le croire, fut le vrai fondateur de la société civile.*'[40] Courts have much difficulty in dealing with this injustice. They lack a criterion to deal with the conflict between a land claim by an indigenous people, whose forefathers were removed a long time ago, and the current owners. Even if they assume there is such a thing as a 'native title',[41] they need the help of the legislator to give effect to the uneasy practical consequences following from this.

The forte of property law lies somewhere else. Though it lacks the instruments to achieve just outcomes across generations, it excels in providing detailed rules on when ownership passes by way of voluntary transfer. This is hardly a surprise: the market economy informing the rules on property law is only able to function if goods can circulate freely. This is not only the reason for the European Union's painstaking efforts to eliminate obstacles to trade among its member states, it also explains why the law is reluctant to allow the seller to prohibit the buyer from alienating the good to somebody else. Law and economics

---

39 Montesquieu 1748, XXVI, 15.
40 Rousseau 1755, 95: 'The first man who, having fenced a piece of land, said "This is mine", and found people naïve enough to believe him, that man was the true founder of civil society'.
41 As the High Court of Australia ruled in *Mabo v Queensland (No. 2)* [1992] HCA 23 1993.

scholars take this insight to extremes by considering property rights as nothing but background rules awaiting reallocation through contract.[42]

The detailed rules on how property is transferred are a comparative lawyer's paradise. They differ significantly from one jurisdiction to another,[43] though often for no other reason than historical accident. The first great divide concerns the time at which the property is transferred. In consensual systems, as exist in France and England, the property passes at the time when the contract is concluded. In traditional systems, such as German and Polish law, the mere sale or donation is not enough and actual delivery of the goods is needed. The second divide concerns the proprietary effect of an underlying defect in the agreement. As was noted in Chapter 2, a party is sometimes able to invalidate a contract for reason of fraud or incapacity. This raises the question whether, upon invalidation, the property automatically returns to the seller. This is indeed the case in so-called causal systems such as French and Dutch law. French and Dutch lawyers reason that with the demise of the justification for the property transfer (usually the sales contract) the property has in retrospect always been with the seller. Abstract systems, such as German law, are based on a different perception. § 929 of the German Civil Code, taking its cue directly from Von Savigny, deliberately omits any reference to the underlying contract. It states: '[f]or the transfer of the ownership of a movable thing, it is necessary that the owner delivers the thing to the acquirer and both agree that ownership is to pass . . .'. As the latter agreement refers to a separate 'real agreement' aimed at transferring the property – a view once hailed as the world record in legal abstraction – the buyer remains the owner after the sales contract has been invalidated. The buyer will still be obliged to give back the good under the rules on restitution, but unlike the situation in a causal system, this personal right is not worth a lot in the instance of the buyer's insolvency.

It seems obvious that one needs to have the property right in the goods to be able to transfer it. This was already expressed by the Roman maxim *nemo plus iuris transferre potest quam ipse habet* ('no one can transfer more than he has himself'). And yet, economic necessity sometimes requires a different solution. If I buy a watch in a shop, I should not have to worry about whether the seller actually owns it or stole it from somebody else. Here lies a dilemma for the lawmaker. Should the law protect the original owner, from whom the watch was stolen, or the purchaser in good faith? The American jurist Grant Gilmore has called it one of the most dramatic episodes in legal history that, after centuries of protecting the owner, the good faith purchaser triumphed in the course of the nineteenth century.[44] Commercial parties and consumers being able to purchase goods in possession of the seller without an extensive investigation of who owns these goods is a simple prerequisite of economic life. However, many jurisdictions pose additional requirements to the benefit of the owner. This is the most obvious in English law that only protects the innocent purchaser of goods if the original owner took the risk of the goods being sold without his authority, for example because they were sold by an unauthorised middleman who made it seem he was the real owner. This means that under English law the owner whose goods were stolen will always prevail over the bona fide purchaser.[45] This gives the right incentive to the owner, who is thus deterred from carelessly giving possession of his goods to others.

The focus the current law puts on the power to use, encumber, keep and transfer is still reminiscent of the nineteenth-century view of looking at property from the perspective of the owner. The reverse perspective would be to consider property rights primarily from the viewpoint of the community. If we assume that a just distribution and fair use of resources are to become more important in the years to come, this is an angle worth exploring further.

---

44 Gilmore 1954, 1057.
45 *National Employers Mutual General Insurance Association Ltd v Jones* [1990] 1 AC 24 (HL).

5 Family law

5.1 Introduction

Who can marry? Who must assume responsibility for children? What duties do cohabiting parties have towards one another? These and similar questions are at the core of family law, the field that deals with the legal consequences of intimate relationships. The traditional relationships family law recognises are those between husband and wife and between parent and child, but in the last few decades family law has greatly expanded its grasp and now also includes the regulation (or deliberate lack thereof) of, for example, relationships between same-sex partners, cohabitants, and sperm donors and their genetic children. The expansion of family law to this wider range of relationships reflects the law's willingness to take the increasing diversity of modern family life into account.

This increasing attention to a great variety of relationships makes the term 'family law' somewhat misleading. The real question here is what we owe to those whom we love, those with whom we live or those with whom we share genetic ties. These obligations are not only of a financial nature but also relate to duties to protect, care and support others. Some have spoken of 'family law exceptionalism': unlike the market, families are about intimate, affective and vulnerable relationships.[1] Interestingly, the emergence of a separate field of study of these relationships only took place in the nineteenth century when German scholars, headed by Von Savigny, 'invented' family law and placed it opposite the law of contract.[2] Unlike the market-driven and 'universal' contract law, essentially the same everywhere, each nation's family law, altruistic and dutiful, would be the unique manifestation of the spirit of a people. Also unlike contract law, these domestic relationships would, in Von Savigny's view, be primarily shaped by the

---

1 Halley and Rittich 2010, 754.
2 Kennedy 2010.

inalterable status of people. Husband, father and son were inescapable life-forms, determined independent of the individual will, destined to endure until death, and with clear obligations under mandatory law.[3]

If Von Savigny was right with his market/family dichotomy, this book could easily have done without this chapter. Family relationships would have belonged to the field of public law, where rights and obligations originate independent of the human will. In today's family law nothing could be further from the truth. If there is anything reflecting people's self-determination, it is their fundamental freedom to choose the partner they love, divorce the partner they are fed up with and raise the children they decide to make. The law must not only give effect to these choices, and the responsibilities they generate, but also protect vulnerable family members. The state's long-time disinterest in family matters, motivated by the wish not to interfere in the family, often caused the continuing abuse of women and children. The need for balancing individual autonomy against other public aims is thus just as important in family law as it is in other areas of private law.

This does not mean that family law is not exceptional in other ways. More so than the rest of private law, it is a showground for political and religious struggles. This is in no small part caused by the shaky assumptions it makes about what is best for society and what people ought to do. For example, should the law aim to strengthen families and therefore encourage people to marry and have children?[4] This is, in fact, a policy in many countries giving tax breaks or benefits to families, based on the idea that they must be preferred over other (single-person) households. However, it is not self-evident this is the proper approach. The survival of the human race is in any event not dependent on a stable bond between a man and a woman, apart from the fact that today's world would probably be better off with a lower birth-rate. It is equally debated whether a two-parent family with parents of opposite sex is the preferred setting for procreation and child rearing. This calls for insight into the psychological development of children. One influential, yet contested, theory developed by English psychiatrist John Bowlby – himself raised by nannies before being sent off to boarding school – indeed claims it is much more important for a child's development to have a single and permanent caregiver to whom the child can attach and develop a bond of love with, than it is to have

---

3 Von Savigny 1840–49, Vol. 1, 46, 284.
4 Glendon 1989, 291 ff; Dewar 2003, 423.

both a mother and a father.[5] This psychological parent need not be a blood relative. Insights like these do not always sit easily together with conventional and religious views of what a family should be about. It is unfortunately easier to say than to realise that the law should not be bothered too much by these 'moral' views and adopt a morally neutral stance towards family issues.[6]

Another aspect making family law special is the mobility of the individuals for whom it seeks to set norms. People cross borders even more frequently than goods or services. This, combined with some countries' hostility towards other countries' solutions for sensitive issues can form an explosive amalgam. For example, must France accept the Islamic divorce obtained by a husband in Morocco which greatly discriminates against the interest of the wife now living in France? And must Indonesia recognise the same-sex marriage of a Dutch couple residing on Kuta Beach? In theory the answer is easy: it is in every country's interest to respect the administrative and judicial decisions of other countries. This is a matter of reciprocity: only if a jurisdiction gives full faith and credit to the judgment of the other jurisdiction will the latter be willing to accept the judgment of the first jurisdiction. This principle of mutual recognition is exactly what is codified in the EU–Brussels II Regulation concerning jurisdiction and the recognition and enforcement of judgments in matrimonial matters and the matters of parental responsibility.[7] However, respect for foreign law ends when it conflicts with the own legal system's fundamental values. This explains why many countries do not recognise a foreign same-sex marriage, including a range of European countries that see no reason to apply the Brussels II Regulation to spouses of the same sex. In this respect Europe is lagging behind the United States, where the couple's state of residence must now accept the same-sex marriage concluded in another state.[8]

5.2   Marriage and cohabitation

For a long time marriage was the central institution in family law. It determined not only the status of the two spouses but also that of

---

5 Bowlby 1969.

6 As propagated by Posner 1992, 85.

7 EU-Regulation 2201/2003 (Brussels II bis).

8 *Obergefell v Hodges*, 576 US _ (2015); see further Section 5.2.1.

children: a child not born within marriage was regarded as 'illegiti-mate'. At a time when marriage was supposed to last till death, divorce rates were low and the great majority of children were in fact born within marriage, society could uphold this view. This time has passed. In the Western world half of marriages end in divorce and around 40 per cent of children in Europe and the United States are born to unmarried couples. In addition, only a minority of households consists of married couples, with or without children. These major changes in family life since the 1960s have had a drastic impact on family law, which is continuously struggling to catch up with the changing concept of the family unit. And, although the general trend has been towards equality, solidarity and recognition of other relationships than marriage this does not mean that the law on these issues is settled. This section deals with two questions: how should the state regulate mar-riage (if at all) and how should it deal with other intimate relationships such as cohabitation?

The discussion of these two questions must be preceded by considering an even more fundamental point: why would people want to get mar-ried or create some other form of partnership at all? Despite romantic ideals about true love and eternal bonds, the main reason for people to share their lives is that it allows for swapping. Cohen puts it like this:

> [M]en and women have much that they can exchange with one another. Each has sex to offer ... Each had procreation to offer ... Then there is physical protection and income (and) homemaking and child rearing ... The central point is that men and women each desire the other as providers of vital services ...[9]

Marriage thus enables the spouses to pool resources and share the costs of cohabitation and child rearing. This is nothing new and clearly serves an evolutionary goal. Anthropologist Helen Fisher spoke about the 'sex contract': because compared to other species the raising of a human child is a long and costly process, women gave sexual exclu-sivity in exchange for food hunted by men and protection of both her and her child.[10] The faint shadow of this in today's society is one partner specialising in earning the family income and the other doing more in the household. The only change with times past is that the evolutionary ratio now also applies to same-sex couples who, thanks

9 Cohen 2000, 13; Cf. Ertman 2015, 487.
10 Fisher 1982, 89.

to modern reproduction techniques, are able to have and raise children as well.

5.2.1   Why regulate marriage and how?

Despite the demise of marriage as the only socially accepted way of demonstrating exclusive and permanent commitment to a partner, marriage remains important. In a recent American case it was described as 'a keystone of our social order' and as an institution embodying the highest ideals of love, fidelity, devotion, sacrifice and family.[11] And yet, it is not self-evident why the state should intervene in regulating, or even promoting, this private vow par excellence. It must be remembered that for a long time in history marriage was purely a religious or a private matter that did not require any official ceremony or registration. This invokes the question of what is actually the public purpose of marriage and why it could not be completely privatised. Pleas in this direction are regularly made. Feminist Naomi Wolf, for example, makes the following point: '[i]n spite of the dress and the flowers, marriage is a business contract . . . Celebrate marriage with a religious or emotional ceremony – leave the State out of it – and create a business- or domestic-partner contract'.[12] So what is it that justifies public marriage?[13]

An often heard voice is that the state should encourage people to marry because it would lead to a more stable relationship and therefore to a better environment for raising children. The state should therefore provide married couples with benefits in taxation, welfare, pensions and inheritance. This argument of channelling[14] people towards participation in a desirable social institution obviously overlooks that stable relationships are not dependent on having walked down the aisle. It is true that statistics show that children in one parent families are more likely to fail at school and become unemployed. However, this does not say much if these statistics at the same time indicate – as they do – that couples who do get married are simply wealthier and can offer their children better prospects in life. The state must therefore have less morally attuned motives for regulating marriage.

---

11 Justice Kennedy in *Obergefell v Hodges*, 576 US _ (2015), at 28.

12 *The Sunday Times* 22 March 2009. See also, www.beyondmarriage.org.

13 Herring, Probert and Gilmore 2015, 165 ff.

14 Schneider 1992.

A more convincing argument is that the state should provide a mechanism through which partners can send a signal to society about their
exclusive mutual commitment.[15] A public marriage ceremony arguably serves this goal better than a private contract or a religious ceremony. The signal it sends is that the two spouses have the intention
to stay together for better or for worse and until death does them part.
The simple fact that the state approves of their relationship is thus
for many a more powerful sign than a mere contract or private vow.
This explains why many same-sex couples are not just satisfied with a
civil (or 'registered') partnership, as is now available in many jurisdictions, but want to obtain what is in their view the ultimate form of
intimate commitment. In this regard, marriage is a marker of social
acceptance.[16]

Another argument for public marriage is that it offers couples the possibility to easily opt into a pre-set bundle of rights and responsibilities.
This not only avoids the drafting of elaborate nuptial agreements but
also allows each individual partner to rely on the protective rules the
law offers on the financial consequences of divorce. In this respect
spouses are not any different than normal contracting parties in need
of both being facilitated by default rules and being protected by mandatory law. Viewed from the perspective of the state, marriage also
has the advantage that because it needs registration it is much easier
to attach consequences to it than to cohabitation. It will be shown, for
example, that it is a highly efficient method of establishing parental
responsibilities.

If marriage has indeed these two public benefits, it does not yet answer
the question of how it should be regulated. Two questions require
attention: to whom should marriage be available and to what extent do
the spouses have freedom in setting their own rights and obligations?

The answer to the first question has long been determined by the
Christian tradition in which marriage is the lawful union of a man and
a woman. As long as spouses are of the opposite sex, all that is required
to marry is that the partners are adults, not closely related or married to
somebody else and freely consenting to the marriage. The law does not
consider whether the marriage is concluded for a good reason: the state
will not check whether the partners love each other, have sex with each

---

15 Posner 2000, 71.
16 Herring, Probert and Gilmore 2015, 169.

other, are faithful or really intend to be married for life. While any other approach aiming to regulate the actual behaviour of the spouses would interfere too much with their right to privacy – let alone that it would be nigh impossible to investigate for the wedding officiant – this may pose a problem in cases where people only marry for reasons of inheritance or gaining access to the country of their desire. States' efforts to try to limit these marriages of convenience are usually to no avail.

A much contested question is whether marriage should also be open to same-sex couples. A religious view of marriage denies this but the key question is why this view should inform a state's concept of marriage. It is not the case that because Christians or Muslims have a particular view of marriage that the law must share it. It is not *their* marriage being offered by the state. What is more, if the public aim of marriage indeed lies in allowing lovers to signal their commitment to the outside world and to facilitate them in the choice they wish to make, it is not clear why same-sex couples should not also be allowed to 'opt in' to this institution. This simply follows from everyone's right to autonomy, or as US Supreme Court judge Warren held in the famous case of *Loving v Virginia*: 'the freedom to marry has long been recognized as one of the vital personal rights essential to the orderly pursuit of happiness by free men'.[17] Warren was not asked to judge about same-sex marriage but in 2015 the court took up the marker he left when it declared the right to personal choice regarding marriage inherent to individual autonomy.[18] As everyone should have this autonomy, allowing same-sex marriage is simply a matter of equal protection. In the pictorial language of justice, Albie Sachs, in yet another case, decided by the Constitutional Court of South Africa, said that the exclusion of same-sex couples from marriage

> represents a harsh if oblique statement by the law that same-sex couples are outsiders . . . It reinforces the wounding notion that they are to be treated as biological oddities, as failed or lapsed human beings who do not fit into normal society, and, as such, do not qualify for the full moral concern and respect that our Constitution seeks to secure for everyone.[19]

Same-sex couples' fundamental right to marry, as is now recognised by the highest courts of the United States and South Africa, is not

---

17 388 US 1, 12 (1967).

18 *Obergefell v Hodges*, 576 US _ (2015).

19 *Minister of Home Affairs v Fourie* 2006 (1) SA 524.

accepted by the European Court of Human Rights. The court considers homosexuals' right to marry as an evolving right the recognition of which falls within the margin of appreciation of each individual state.[20] Only a few European countries, such as France, Sweden, Spain and the Netherlands, have introduced same-sex marriage by way of statute. This surely does not end the marriage debate. If one is willing to set aside the romantic, cultural and religious notion of marriage, it is difficult to see why it could not simply be replaced with a new public institution that promotes any intimate relationship of care.[21] The fidelity, support and assistance spouses promise each other could, after all, also extend to relationships among children and their aging parents, cohabitating unmarried sisters or close friends taking care of each other. Such a 'sexless' family law, as Herring calls it, would push marriage into the realm of the private again.

The second question is to what extent spouses should have autonomy in creating their own marriage arrangements. Put differently: does marriage primarily provide a status, or is it a contract of which the terms can be set by the spouses? Apart from pre-nuptial agreements about the financial aspects of marriage and divorce, the current law does not allow much contractual freedom. Spouses have to say 'yes' to a fixed package in which the conditions for entry and exit and benefits and responsibilities are strictly defined. In this sense, the old US Supreme Court's qualification of marriage as an institution that cannot be modified, restricted, enlarged or released upon the consent of the parties is still valid.[22] This has the obvious advantage of the richer and more powerful spouse (often the husband) not being able to contract away the protection the law offers to his less potent partner. But if one regards marriage as an egalitarian liberal community of two equal people,[23] it is not clear why the spouses should not be allowed some more autonomy. This is why the states of Louisiana and Arizona allow future spouses to conclude a so-called 'covenant marriage' that only allows divorce in cases of fault, thus limiting the spouses' right to exit to an even greater extent than normal marriage does.

If these more binding marriage commitments are put at the disposal of partners, it is difficult to see why states should not also allow other

---

20 *Schalk and Kopf v Austria*, No. 30141/04, [2010] ECHR 995; *Oliari and others v Italy*, Nos. 18766/11 and 36030/11.

21 Herring 2013; Fineman 1995.

22 *Maynard v Hill*, 125 US 190, 211 (1888).

23 Frantz and Dagan 2004.

types of customised marriage. These could range from a 'parenting marriage' contract or an 'open marriage contract' to agreements on sex, visiting in-laws or the religion in which future children will be raised. Even if courts may not enforce such clauses, they still shape the spouses' expectations and empower them to make moral commitments. The suggestion has also been made to allow for a fixed term or 'starter' marriage. This could last for three or five years, after which the couple can decide whether to renew the contract. Such a temporary marriage exists in Islamic law (*Mutah*), where it is arguably only a means to legalise sexual intercourse by men married to somebody else on a more permanent basis. But the advantage of taking the 'till death us do part' vow out of Western marriage is that spouses can try out the institution, as well as each other, and are likely to have a more amicable divorce in cases where the 'wedlease' ends anyway.[24]

While under the current law most spouses have thus little to choose when it comes to the form, length and contents of their marriage, the question is whether they should have more autonomy in matters of property. Are spouses allowed to provide for the consequences marriage has on their assets? The answer is in the affirmative but whether they also *need* to do so depends entirely on the statutory default regime applicable to the proprietary consequences of marriage. In most common law jurisdictions, including England and a majority of US states, marriage does not affect the ownership of assets and potential debts of the spouses at all. Assets and debts from before marriage, as well as what spouses acquire or come to owe during marriage, are attributed to each of them. They are of course free to put property in the name of both spouses but if they do not, each will remain the sole owner as if they are not married.

Other jurisdictions apply a regime of limited community property. In France and Russia, for example, any individual assets acquired during marriage belong to the couple together, while both spouses are liable for debts contracted by only one of them. Pre-existing property (in most cases no more than some tangible goods and a bank account) as well as gifts and inheritances remain separate.[25] Similar 'community of acquisitions' regimes can be found in a wide range of other jurisdictions, including China, California and Texas. Germany's 'community of accrued gains' keeps spouses' property separate during marriage

---

24 Gadoua and Larson 2014.
25 The *Communauté des acquêts* of Art. 1401 French *Code Civil*.

but obliges each spouse upon divorce to compensate the other for the accrued gains.[26] All these variations on a common theme make a lot of sense: the newly shared life should not affect pre-existing assets or debts, but as soon as people marry they start to participate in an economic unit legitimising the mixing of their property or, in any event, a claim upon divorce on what the other spouse built up.[27] This also comes out in the fact that, even in jurisdictions with a full separation of ownership, selling or mortgaging the family home always requires the consent of the other spouse, while debts incurred to run the household and raise the children are always joint even in cases where only one of the spouses took on the obligation. A minority of jurisdictions, including the Netherlands and South Africa, apply a third type of regime in which a full common property pool is formed at marriage regardless of when (before or after marriage) assets were acquired or debts were contracted.

The amount of autonomy left to spouses in overriding these default matrimonial property regimes is dependent on their motives for doing so. One obvious motive is to provide for the financial consequences of divorce. It will be shown (Section 5.4.3) that the law is generally suspicious of this motive and strictly scrutinises marital agreements by way of 'pre- or post-nups' with a view to maintaining the solidarity ex-partners owe each other. Another motive, and one playing an important role in community property regimes, is to protect a spouse from the creditors of the other spouse during marriage. If the wife is self-employed and regularly incurs financial risks, spouses will wish to avoid that creditors can take recourse on all common assets including those brought into the community from the side of the husband. The law considers this a perfectly legitimate motive. One may even wonder whether the default regime is in this respect not inadequate: why should it matter to the creditor that the debtor is married, thus accidentally providing an extra resource?[28]

5.2.2   Cohabitation

Many couples decide not to get married or enter into a civil (or 'registered') partnership but are perfectly happy living under one roof.

---

26 The *Zugewinngemeinschaft* of § 1363 BGB.

27 Cf. Art. 4.35 Principles of European Family Law (PEFL) regarding Property Relations between Spouses (2013) (see www.ceflonline.net/principles) and American Law Institute Principles of the Law of Family Dissolution § 4.03 (2002).

28 Verbeke 2001, 392.

They can do so for different reasons. Many cohabitants intend to stay together for the rest of their lives but do not see the need to formalise this or simply find marriage a small-minded institution. It could also be that they want to 'try out' their relationship, while other cohabitants simply share a household for the sake of convenience without regarding the partner as the love of their life. This variety of relationships makes it difficult to define cohabitation.[29] Is 'staying over' every weekend enough? Does 'living apart together' also qualify? And how about the relationship between an older woman and her live-in-lover? In so far as legislators and courts provide special rules for cohabitation they tend to emphasise that the partners must have a continuous and intimate relationship and form a common household.

The law finds it difficult to deal with cohabitation. If the law would treat two unmarried lovers who break up after 30 years as legal strangers, it may be that one of them (typically the woman) is left out in the cold. A standard situation is that partner A moves into partner B's house, who is the sole owner of the property. They live together and have children. Partner A has no right to a share of the property when they break up after 15 years, despite the fact that she may have contributed to paying the mortgage or stayed at home to run the common household and raise the children. Partner A is also not entitled to any maintenance or inheritance claims. She could even get evicted from the family home.

One solution to this problem is to treat the couple as if they are married. If two people eat, drink and sleep together why not equalise their relationship with marriage? This solution has deep historical roots in the common law world. Some common law jurisdictions, including nine states in the United States, accept a so-called 'common-law marriage'. This means that a couple is legally considered married without any formal ceremony or registration, provided the partners regard themselves as married and hold themselves out as husband and wife to the outside world. Jurisdictions that do not accept this somewhat peculiar legal institution could still treat cohabitation on the same footing as marriage. This is, for example, the case in the Canadian province of Saskatchewan, which for the sake of maintenance, pensions, property and homestead defines not only a married person as 'spouse' but also either of two persons who 'is cohabiting or has cohabited with the other person as spouses continuously for a period of not less than two years'.[30]

---

29 Herring 2014, 20; Probert 2012, 4 ff.
30 S. 2 Family Property Act.

This approach is not necessarily the best one. It negates the possibility of parties having made the deliberate choice *not* to get married or enter into a civil partnership out of dislike for its consequences. It is likely that an increasing number of people, in particular women, refrain from getting married because the divorce regime offers too little protection for the investments and sacrifices they make during marriage.[31] In this respect, Saskatchewan makes a major inroad on party autonomy. The counter-argument is that partners could have made a cohabitation agreement on the costs of the common household and what happens with jointly purchased assets in the case of separation. A fair and more nuanced solution is therefore one that protects the weaker partner while still respecting the couple's common intention. In the absence of the couple's clear and well-informed choice for any other division, there is much to say in favour of an equal split in the case of a long-standing cohabitation with one partner earning the income and the other contributing to home-making and upbringing the children after having given up paid work. This would only be another illustration of the fact that property in a domestic context is different from property in a commercial context.

5.3   Parents and parental responsibilities

Article 16 of the 1948 Universal Declaration of Human Rights provides men and women of full age with the fundamental right to marry and found a family. Thanks to the wide availability of contraception and abortion the decision to have children and decide upon the size of the family is, in today's world, indeed a matter of choice and not of biological destiny – never better described than in Nina Hagen's exclamation '*Ich hab' keine Pflicht*'.[32] Many regard the decision whether or not to procreate as the most momentous of human choices and therefore as the ultimate in self-determination. This becomes even clearer if one realises that the decision to have children is necessarily a selfish one. Most prospective parents find it difficult to explain why they decide to have a child. Motives range from creating a companion and living on in the next generation to overcoming mortality, cementing a marriage, guaranteeing support when growing old or serving their God. These

---

31 Dnes 2002, 129.
32 'I don't have any duty': Nina Hagen, 'Unbeschreiblich Weiblich' (from the album *Nina Hagen Band*, 1978).

are all motives not in the immediate interests of the child itself.[33] An ethicist would argue that future children have no entitlement to come into existence.[34] All this changes once the child is born. The child is in need of food, clothes and shelter, proper education and representation in matters of property and medical treatment. This is where the concern of private law lies: it must decide who should be in charge of safeguarding the welfare of the child until it has reached the age of majority. This is a wide-ranging responsibility: it extends to feeding and changing diapers of infants to providing adequate housing, clothing, education and a safe and nurturing environment. Even if the child does not live with them, parents still have the obligation to provide financial and material support.

Parental responsibilities are by default entrusted to the child's (biological) parents. The presumption is that they are in the best position to protect the interests of their children, whom they usually know best and almost invariably feel a strong attachment to. This means that parenthood is not dependent on parental fitness. While future drivers have to obtain a driver's licence and there is a minimum age to marry or to buy alcohol everybody is allowed to raise their own children. A parent will only be discharged in the highly exceptional case in which his or her behaviour or neglect causes a serious risk to the person or the property of the child.[35] This is a low standard that in many countries still allows feeding a child until it is obese and rejecting vaccinations or blood transfusions in the case of illness. What is more, in the case of a child who has been subject to serious maltreatment the harm has already been done.

This explains why some argue in favour of a less parent-centric approach. Probably the most extreme proposal is to *ex ante* identify parents who are not able to act in the child's best interests because they are drug addicts or economically and socially deprived. If these parents are likely to be discharged from parenthood after bad things happened, would it then not be better to hand their babies over to more able child-rearers upon birth?[36] Identifying suitable parents is, after all, what already happens in cases of adoption. Provided one is able to identify bad parents in advance – which is in fact highly problematic –

---

33 Barton and Douglas 1995, 22.
34 Overall 2012.
35 As stated in Art. 3:32 PEFL regarding Parental Responsibilities (2007).
36 Dwyer 2011, 191 ff; Eisenberg 1994, 416.

such a system of 'licenced parenting' would surely advance the cause of protecting children. But society would also regard it as a grave violation of the parents' personal freedom. One court found that there is a 'private realm of family life which the state cannot enter'.[37] Another court reasoned that 'the best person to bring up a child is the natural parent. It matters not whether the parent is wise or foolish, rich or poor, educated or illiterate. Public authorities cannot improve on nature'.[38] And indeed: in the absence of one uniform view of what parenting should be about, autonomy in family affairs is probably the only thing that keeps us from a totalitarian state. This also explains why many have a natural dislike of the collective upbringing of children as practised in, for example, the Israeli Kibbutz and the Bhagwan ashram.[39]

If the best interests of the child prevail in matters of parental responsibility, should the child not be allowed to make his or her own decisions in accordance with its developing understanding and abilities?[40] This question goes to the heart of the contested issue of children's rights. While the 1989 United Nations Convention on the Rights of the Child allows a child to express his or her views in important matters, it does not give children the autonomy to decide these matters for themselves. The rationale is that children could otherwise endanger their own health or development. This is particularly critical when the view of the child differs from that of the parents. Can a 12 year old enforce its preference for a vegan lifestyle against the will of its parents who fear their child will end up looking like a scarecrow? And is a 15-year-old girl allowed to receive contraception from a doctor without her parents' knowledge or consent? The English court held that, despite her Catholic mother's objections, she is if she has sufficient understanding and intelligence to know what contraception involves.[41] The convincing underlying motive is that parental rights to control a child do not exist to please the parents, but are there for the benefit of the child.

It was noted above that parental responsibilities do not necessarily lie with the biological parents. Children could be adopted, be raised by a step-parent or taken into care (which usually means they are placed

---

37 *Prince v Massachusetts*, 321 US 158, 166 (1944).
38 *Re K(D) (a Minor)* [1988] AC 806, 812 (HL) *per* Lord Templeman.
39 Following the lead of Plato's *Republic*, Book V, 460.
40 Cf. Art. 3.4 PEFL regarding Parental Responsibilities (2007).
41 In *Gillick v West Norfolk and Wisbech Area and Dept of Health* [1986] 1 AC 112.

within a family of foster carers). In most cases the woman giving birth to a child will be regarded as the mother while the mother's husband (or civil partner) is presumed to be the father. In the case of a mother who is not married or in a civil partnership, somebody else (usually, but not necessarily, the biological father) can recognise the child, or establish a parental status pre or post birth. All this may seem too obvious for words but one must realise that until quite recently children born out of wedlock were regarded as illegitimate. Such children were not only deprived of the rights other children did have (e.g., on maintenance and inheritance), many a jurisdiction did not even create an automatic legal bond between an unmarried mother and child at birth. Children were also stigmatised by society, of which the word 'bastard' is still a living memory. Equality of children born in and outside of matrimony was only reached in the 1970s when both the US Supreme Court and the European Court of Human Rights[42] declared the notion of illegitimate children contrary to fundamental rights.

The rise of assisted reproductive technologies such as in-vitro fertilisation (IVF) and embryo transplantation poses a special problem for establishing parenthood. When, in 1983, the first child conceived by donor egg-IVF was born, even the most venerable of family law maxims, namely *Mater semper certa est* ('the mother is always certain'), could no longer be applied. The legislator's reaction that it is not the genetic mother who is the mother of the child but the woman who gives birth to it[43] only offers a solution for those cases in which the latter is indeed the intending mother. This is not always the case and in reality many complicated situations arise as a result of assisted reproduction. The law's concern here is to reduce uncertainty about the legal status of those who take care of the child and of those who have provided the genetic materials for that child. The general trend is that in these cases the role of biology and genetics in establishing parenthood is replaced with a mix of the parties' intent and the child's best interests. Reproductive autonomy – the ability to make one's own decisions about reproduction – thus does not only extend to the decision of whether to have a child or not (including the right to use contraception, to abortion and to have the child adopted) but also affects the previously pure public law issue of who is a parent.[44]

---

42 *Marckx v Belgium*, No. 6833/74, [1979] 2 ECHR 330.
43 See, e.g., § 1591 BGB; Art. 1:198 Dutch Civil Code; Uniform Parentage Act (US) s. 201.
44 Nelson 2013, 2.

An example of the increased role of reproductive autonomy can be seen in the case of surrogacy arrangements. The use of a surrogate mother to bear children for somebody else is as such nothing new. The Old Testament tells us about Sarah who had not become pregnant from her husband Abraham. She therefore gave her Egyptian servant Hagar to Abraham and told him: 'Go, sleep with my slave; perhaps I can build a family through her'.[45] In today's world surrogacy does often not consist of this traditional type (in which the child is genetically related to the surrogate mother), but concerns so-called gestational surrogacy. This means that – usually – IVF is used to transfer an already conceived embryo to the gestational carrier who consequently has no genetic ties to the newborn. The intention of the parents is that the default rules on parenthood are set aside through agreement between the intending parents and the woman who agrees to bear and give birth to the child. This surrogacy agreement is the key element: it obliges the carrier to give up the child that subsequently – with the necessary help of the relevant authorities – will be put under the parental responsibility of the intending parents. Section 801 of the American Uniform Parentage Act (a model law now adopted in 11 states) puts it succinctly like this: '[t]he intended parents become the parents of the child'. The surrogate mother may be given visitation rights.[46] However, not all jurisdictions follow this moderately liberal lead. Some (such as India and Ukraine) even allow commercial surrogacy, while others (including France) ban surrogacy completely. In many other countries the legal position is unclear, much to the detriment of all parties involved. A court in California rightly held:

> No matter what one thinks of artificial insemination, traditional and gestational surrogacy ... and – as now appears in the not-too-distant future, cloning and even gene splicing – courts are still going to be faced with the problem of determining lawful parentage. A child cannot be ignored. Even if all means of artificial reproduction were outlawed with draconian criminal penalties visited on the doctors and parties involved, courts will still be called upon to decide who the lawful parents really are and who – other than the taxpayers – is obligated to provide maintenance and support for the child. These cases will not go away.[47]

The legal prohibition of surrogacy (and of certain reproductive techniques) in some countries, and its wide availability in others, has given

---

45 Genesis 16:2.
46 As in the famous *Baby M* case of the Supreme Court of New Jersey: 109 N.J. 396 (1988).
47 *In re Marriage of Bucanza* 61 Cal. App. 4th 1428 (1998).

rise to so-called fertility tourism: the practice of intending parents to select a surrogate mother for their children by traveling to a surrogacy-friendly destination and take the newborn home from there. Some countries deliberately promote this practice by providing unequivocal rules on who becomes a parent. The Family Code of Ukraine, for example, contains the comforting provision that 'if an ovum conceived by the spouses is implanted to another woman, the spouses shall be the parents of the child'.[48] This will still require the parents' country of residence (or citizenship) to recognise this, but many countries will do so because any other solution is not likely to be in the best interests of the newborn in the longer term. The ethical (and public policy) question in the background is, of course, whether these arrangements are indeed a matter of women determining their own reproductive rights and autonomy ('women helping women') or the exploitation of poor women being abused as birth mothers.

5.4   Divorce and its consequences

5.4.1   Dissolution of marriage

If marriage is based on the mutual consent of the partners, what is more understandable than that they should also be able to exit from their commitment? The case for the free and unilateral availability of divorce (and dissolution in the case of a civil partnership) can be made with even more vigour than in the case of a 'normal' contract. This is because intimacy is particularly valuable when voluntarily chosen.[49] The whole idea of marriage would be undermined if spouses are forced to stay together when tenderness and affection have been replaced with conflict and hatred.

However, this is not the position of the law. The law of most states makes divorce difficult and has two reasons for doing so: a bad one and a good one. The bad reason is vested in history and tradition. If marriage is for better or for worse and destined to last for life, there is no need to make termination readily available. Until the 1950s most married women had little to choose anyway: divorce would require them to live apart from their husband and earn their own income, which was often very difficult to realise. The good reason is that a purely consensual divorce could prove a risk to the interests of the more

---

48 Art. 123(2).
49 Frantz and Dagan 2004, 87.

vulnerable partner and potential children. In traditional marriage, with the husband earning money and the wife taking care of the children and the family home, the wife has a legitimate expectation to share in the husband's financial success, also after divorce.[50] But the wish of the spouse to get out of an unhappy marriage could gravely affect her ability to look after her own interests. The interests of potential children would also have to be assessed. This speaks against a quick and easy exit and justifies intervention of a court in setting the terms of the divorce.

The above pleads in favour of an unlimited right to divorce provided that the court or some other authority is able to rule on child custody and support, distribution of property and alimony. Yet, many jurisdictions still require a more substantive test. Until the 1970s[51] a 'matrimonial offence' (such as adultery) had to be proven, while today the dissolution of marriage is usually made dependent on an irretrievable marital breakdown. What this means exactly depends on the jurisdiction, but a not uncommon requirement is that the couple has lived apart for a set period of one[52] or two years.[53] It is difficult to see the justification for this: one does not leave a husband or a wife lightheartedly and to keep people trapped in a marriage they want to get out of seems intrusive on their personal autonomy. This also refutes the argument that liberalisation of divorce law would lead to more divorces. This is true in fact – if divorce is not allowed, as is the case in the Philippines, the divorce rate is 0 per cent – but it tells us nothing about how happy people are within their marriage or whether they are in reality living as a couple in a 'family unit'. The current 40 per cent of marriages ending in divorce in industrialised nations seems a more accurate estimate of marriage discontentment.

Divorce is not always of the standard type as just described. It was already observed that some US states allow spouses to agree to a covenant marriage that only allows divorce in cases of fault. Other jurisdictions (including Norway and Portugal) accept that consensual divorce should be possible without judicial intervention, in particular in cases where the couple has no children. Spouses can make use of a

---

50 See Section 5.4.3.

51 California introduced no-fault divorce in 1969, Ireland only in 1997.

52 See, e.g., Art. 1:8 PEFL regarding Divorce and Maintenance between former Spouses (2004); § 1566, s. 2 BGB.

53 As in many states of the United States.

simple administrative procedure after having agreed themselves upon maintenance. Such a settled divorce is still likely to be in line with the existing law: because spouses can foresee what would happen in the case of a judicial decision, this will greatly influence their negotiating behaviour outside the courtroom. They bargain 'in the shadow of the law'.[54]

Yet another type of divorce is the dissolution of a religious marriage such as the *Talaq* under Islamic law or the *Get* under Jewish law. The *Talaq* as practised, for example, in Iran, Saudi-Arabia and Pakistan allows the husband to divorce his wife by three times pronouncing the phrase 'I divorce you' (if need be by using email or WhatsApp). Due to mass migration, Western courts are increasingly confronted with such unilateral divorces and they need to decide whether they want to recognise them. The reverse situation is when the husband refuses to divorce his wife and she then claims before a state court that he must cooperate in dissolving the religious marriage. The man's refusal cannot prevent the wife from concluding a proper civil marriage, but there is a good reason to allow the injunction if remaining bound to the religious marriage would unduly limit the wife in living the life she wants to lead. The inability to re-marry under religious law and the practical impossibility to return to her home country – leaving her husband for another man could lead to the death penalty or stoning – may count as such. This does not mean that the state court is the first instance the woman should turn to. Arguably she is first to address a religious institution such as a sharia council. This council can act as an arbitration tribunal and only if it violates the fundamental principles of the secular legal order by keeping the woman trapped inside her marriage should she be able to turn to the state court.[55]

5.4.2   Disputes over children

The effect of the rise of no-fault divorce is that the law is no longer so much interested in whether divorce should be possible, but more in the effects it should have on the couple's finances and the allocation of parental responsibilities.[56] Unlike the termination of normal contracts, divorce does not usually mean that each of the parties can go their own way and start anew. It only means that affection and a shared family

54 Kornhauser and Mnookin 1979.
55 District Court Rotterdam 6 January 2016, ECLI:NL:RBROT:2016:8 (*Talaq*).
56 Krause 2006, 1113.

life make place for family *law*. The new post-divorce arrangement aims to hold the fragments together by imposing a new legal order on the parties.[57]

Disputes over children are unfortunately a common phenomenon among former spouses or partners. The prevalent principle is that of shared parenting: both parents will jointly exercise the parental responsibility for their common children.[58] This means that they have to take the important decisions such as those affecting education, medical treatment and administration of the child's property together. Only in exceptional cases will custody be awarded to one parent, for example in cases where the other parent can no longer be reached, is mentally unstable or if there is a risk for the child to get lost in between the squabbles of its parents. Also, the principle of shared parenting does not say anything about with whom the child will primarily live ('residence') and how often the other parent is allowed to have access to the child ('contact'). In both matters the standard is again that of the best interests of the child. This standard is used in virtually every jurisdiction as well as in the United Nations Convention on the Rights of the Child.[59]

The primary residence of the child is usually with one of the parents. Ideally the ex-partners agree among themselves with whom their child will live. If they cannot reach an agreement, the court decides taking into account the child's wishes and emotional needs, the stability of the home, the physical and mental health of the parents and their availability. In particular the last factor tends to lead to the child living with his or her mother. In the last decade legislators have not been insensitive to the idea – also expressed by fathers' rights advocacy movements – that shared parenting must also mean shared residence. This would entail that the child spends half its time with the father and half with the mother. However, the question is whether such a shared residence arrangement is not more in the interest of the parents than in that of the child.[60] It is not likely that infants will benefit from shared residence. In the case of older children much depends on the relationship between the parents and the distance at which they live from each other: one does not want the child to change school in the middle of the week.

---

57 Smart and Neale 1999, 181.

58 See, e.g., Art. 3.11 PEFL regarding Parental Responsibilities (2007).

59 Art. 3: 'In all actions concerning children . . . the best interests of the child shall be a primary consideration'.

60 Herring, Probert and Gilmore 2015, 90 ff.

Once it is established with whom the child will live, the other parent is usually given 'contact' with the child. Visitation often means that the child spends weekends and part of the holidays with the non-resident parent. However, the court's contact order is more easily given than enforced. Sanctioning the resident mother who refuses to send the child to her ex-partner may in practice not be in the child's best interests. Ordering her to pay a fine or even put her in prison could leave the child sandwiched in between the two parents.[61] This is where the power of the law must give in to the messy reality of post-divorce parenting.

A debated question is whether there is also an enforceable right for the parent to have contact with the child. The European Court of Human Rights seemed to eschew the term 'right' when it held that 'the mutual enjoyment by parent and child of each other's company constitutes a fundamental element of family life'.[62] The ultimate criterion is again whether visiting a parent contributes to the child's welfare and in highly exceptional circumstances this may not be the case. If, for example, a child was abused by his or her father and suffers from fear of new domestic violence there is a good reason to temporarily cut the child off from its roots.

5.4.3   Financial consequences

Divorce is one of the main reasons for poverty in industrialised nations. Statistics show that divorced women and single parent families are more likely to have financial problems than any other type of household. This puts into perspective the role that law can play in providing a fair arrangement of the financial consequences of divorce. Yet, this is what the law aims to do. The law's concern here lies with three different issues: child maintenance, maintenance for the ex-partner and division of marital property.

It is the duty of both parents to ensure that their child is fed, clothed and educated and has reasonably sufficient means to grow up. This is why a parent has to support its children usually until they are 21 years old, and in some jurisdictions even beyond that age. This duty does not end upon divorce or, in the case of unmarried parents, separation. Children can be seen as the ultimate common project of the partners

---

61 See Herring 2013, 64.

62 *Gnahoré v France*, No. 40031/98, [2002] 34 ECHR 38.

and this project is not dependent on them staying together.[63] The wish not to leave one partner with all financial burdens is usually translated into ordering the non-resident parent to make a monthly payment for child maintenance. The required amount is mostly based on child maintenance guidelines that use, for example, the average cost of raising children or the percentage of parental income spent on the child before divorce. One reason why this often leaves the resident parent (typically the mother) financially worse off is that the non-resident parent will only be forced to pay if he has sufficient means left to support himself. This will certainly require the debtor to make every possible effort to find a job but it still means that the risk of insufficient finances to bring up the child is shifted to the resident parent. An even bigger problem is poor compliance with child maintenance orders. Some jurisdictions (including the United Kingdom and the Netherlands) have set up government bodies to collect the maintenance if a parent is unwilling to pay. Several US states even revoke the debtor's driver's licence or allow the court to send the non-paying parent to jail. These severe sanctions confirm the interest of society (and therefore of the state) in protecting its most vulnerable citizens from want and in avoiding that the taxpayer ends up paying for the raising of children.

If marriage would be like a normal contract, termination would end the obligations of the spouses. It could be that one spouse needs to pay a sum in damages to the other for breaking up what was supposed to be a lifelong commitment, but this is where the relationship would end. Terminating marriage is clearly different. In many cases the law obliges an ex-partner to support his or her former spouse financially for a set period. However, unlike claims for child support, maintenance claims between spouses are made dependent on the needs of the creditor spouse. The claim will therefore not only fail if the debtor spouse is unable to pay, but also if the creditor has sufficient means or ways to earn money him- or herself. The right to maintenance does not legitimate the creditor to remain inactive. In practice, account will be taken of factors such as spouses' employment abilities, age and health, care of children, division of duties during marriage, duration of marriage, standard of living during marriage and any new long-term relationship.[64] Even future events in the ex-partner's new life can affect the amount the creditor spouse is entitled to: he or she may be able to claim a share if the ex-partner wins the lottery or gets a better job.

---

63 Frantz and Dagan 2004, 89 ff.
64 Cf. Arts. 2.2–2.4 PEFL regarding Divorce and Maintenance between former Spouses (2004).

The key question is why spousal maintenance should exist at all. Should ex-partners not be able to start a new life without the burden of having to pay their ex? The law's motive for redistribution of income upon divorce is the same as for the division of marital property.[65] Reorganising income and assets upon separation simply follows from the previously mentioned nature of marriage as a swap contract. Spouses swap financial support for care of home, hearth and children.[66] They make their career decisions together: one gives up a job or works fewer hours, the other makes a career. In the eyes of the law care, feeding and cleaning are just as important to this partnership as bringing in the family income. Therefore, divorce does not end the legitimate expectation of the spouse (in most cases the wife) to be compensated for her investment. This view of marriage as a common project with financial solidarity is even more important in view of the fact that women in particular suffer high costs when exiting marriage. Economists point out that their value in both the labour and the marriage market is lower after divorce than that of men. It will simply be more difficult for them to find a suitable job and a new partner.

This explains why equal division of property has become the norm in jurisdictions that keep spouses' assets separate during marriage, such as England and most US states.[67] This can be illustrated with the well-known English case of *White v White*.[68] Here a couple had built up assets worth £4.5 million during their 33 years of marriage. In line with the then prevailing law, the lower court had awarded the wife an amount of £800,000 upon divorce based on reasonable needs for the rest of her life. The husband was allowed to keep the rest. The House of Lords rightly replaced this unfair approach with an equal division of assets among the ex-partners. The argument revealed by Lord Nicholls is exactly the one just mentioned:

> Typically, a husband and wife share the activities of earning money, running their home and caring for their children. Traditionally, the husband earned the money, and the wife looked after the home and the children. This traditional division is no longer the order of the day ... But whatever the division of labour chosen by the husband and wife, or forced upon them by

65 This explains why the common law usually clumps maintenance and property division together as one package of financial relief: Herring, Probert and Gilmore 2015, 246 ff.
66 Ertman 2015, 481.
67 See Section 5.2.1.
68 *White v White* [2000] 3 FCR 555.

circumstances, fairness requires that this should not prejudice or advantage either party . . . If, in their different spheres, each contributed equally to the family, then in principle it matters not which of them earned the money and built up the assets. There should be no bias in favour of the money-earner and against the home-maker and the child-carer.

Division of marital property is obviously less acute in a regime of community property, which most jurisdictions adopt. But here another question emerges: what if the spouses decided to opt out of the default matrimonial regime by making a marital agreement? It was noted in Section 5.2.1 that such pre-nups can serve different goals, one of which is to deal with the financial consequences of divorce. There was a time when courts looked at such agreements with great suspicion or even regarded them as contrary to public policy. Their reasoning was that soon-to-weds should not be able even to contemplate divorce and plan to fail.[69] English law essentially adopted this position until 2010.[70] Nowadays most legal systems show more respect for the couple's individual autonomy and recognise that it would be paternalistic and unfair to override their well-considered agreement about what happens to property, and possibly even to pension rights and spousal maintenance, upon divorce. Having said this, courts will still be reluctant to enforce nuptial agreements that in fact only operate as an insurance policy for the wealthier partner who no longer fancies his or her companion. Many jurisdictions are therefore wary to allow a contractual separation of assets negating the financial solidarity among breadwinner and carer. The underlying reason is that financial choices made at the time of marriage are not only likely to be tainted by love and romance, but are also almost never sufficiently informed about what could happen in the future. People cannot contemplate what their position will be after 14 years, being the average length of a marriage before divorce in Organisation for Economic and Co-operation and Development (OECD) countries.

These rules on the financial consequences of divorce are exemplary for the twin focus characterising family law as a whole. While the autonomy of family members in setting their own rules is increasingly recognised – which is just another way of saying that family law has become more individualistic and secular – protection of the vulnerable is equally important.

---

69 Scherpe 2012, 1136.
70 *Radmacher v Granatino* [2010] UKSC 42, 75.

6   Succession law

6.1   Introduction

It is obvious that private ownership lapses upon death. Society therefore needs to decide what it wants to do with the property of the
deceased. The solution of the ancient Egyptians, who took their valuable objects with them in their tomb, is no longer very appealing. In
essence three options exist. The first is to give the state the power to
confiscate the property and to turn it to use for the common good. The
state could then, for example, sell the property and use the proceeds
to finance healthcare or sustainable energy. A second possibility is to
provide rules allocating the property of the deceased to well-defined
groups of people such as family members. The third route is to allow
people to decide for themselves whom they wish to give their assets
to. Which option is best will depend on societal circumstances and on
one's worldview. In fact, writers as renown as Blackstone[1] and Locke[2]
have hailed both the first and the second option as following from
the natural law. The third option seems to fit in best with the view of
private law being about the exercise of individual autonomy. It may
therefore not come as a surprise that all three solutions appeal to dif-
fering aspects we value in life.[3]

The first solution, that of the state reclaiming the deceased's property, appeals to our sense that wealth must be based on merits and
not on the coincidence of having a rich family. Just as it is not seen
as appropriate that family members succeed to public offices or jobs
– heads of state in realms being the remarkable exception – wealth
should not automatically transfer to family. Such a windfall is not only

---

1 Blackstone 1765–69, Book 2, 9: 'the law of nature suggests, that on the death of the possessor the
   estate should again become common, and be open to the next occupant, unless otherwise ordered
   for the sake of civil peace by the positive law of society'.
2 Locke 1689, § I.89: '[n]ature appoints the descent of [dying parents'] property to their children'.
3 Friedman 2009, 15.

undeserved but also runs the risk of jeopardising equality of opportunity through the excessive accumulation of wealth among a small part of the population.[4] Piketty shows this risk has already materialised in Western economies that, precisely as a result of inherited wealth, grow ever more unequal.[5] To use succession law as an instrument of social reform could be a highly effective remedy, but in reality states are highly reluctant to do so. Germany and Italy even give constitutional status to an individual's right to inherit. The closest states get to confiscation is to levy taxes on the value of the property owned by a deceased person. Succession taxes (opponents say 'death tax') at the top rate vary greatly from 55 per cent in Japan to much lower percentages elsewhere. The average top rate in OECD countries is 15 per cent, certainly not enough to tackle Piketty's problem of 'patrimonial capitalism' effectively. But to propose a progressive tax reaching, for example, 100 per cent for inheritances over €1 million will indeed be a sure way for politicians not to get re-elected.

The current law of succession forms a combination of the other two options. It not only allows a person to dispose of his property (so-called testate succession) but also provides default rules for cases in which he does not (intestate succession). Such a mixture of facilitative default rules and the freedom of parties to set these aside was encountered before in this book. The special thing about succession law, however, is that many jurisdictions severely limit this freedom of testation for the sake of protecting family members. The freedom to transfer property *inter vivos* (by way of sale or gift) is usually much greater than that afforded to the disposal of one's assets *mortis causa*. One question to be answered is whether this difference is justified.

6.2   Freedom of testation

Freedom of testation allows a person to dispose of his property upon death. This principle is given effect by allowing people to make a (last) will, or some other type of disposition, in which they prescribe who gets what. Making a will is today often only one element of a more comprehensive process of 'estate planning', through which people aim to maximise the assets to be transferred to designated beneficiaries while paying as little tax as possible. Despite the general acceptance

---

4 Rawls 1971, 63.
5 Piketty 2014, 417.

of testamentary freedom, essential for this type of planning, jurisdictions differ in the types of wills they accept and in the exact limits they pose.[6] This may explain why wills are a regular source of inspiration in television series and detective novels.

The law's main concern with wills (oft-named testaments) is that they express the true intention of the testator. The difficulty is that – unlike what is usually the case with contracting parties – the testator is no longer around to provide information on what he actually meant. This explains why some jurisdictions only allow public wills drafted by a civil law notary, who is supposed to check carefully on the person's intentions and to translate these intentions into proper legalese. In the absence of a civil law notary, common law jurisdictions have no choice but to accept private wills but require that they be signed by witnesses. Other jurisdictions (including Germany and France) accept both public and private wills but then oblige the testator to write the private will in his own hand to prevent falsification. This need not be very complicated. The Guinness Book of Records reports the shortest will ever written to be '*Vse zene*' (Czech for 'all to my wife'), written on the bedroom wall of a man realising his imminent death.

People can have too high expectations of what inheritance law can manage. In one German case the deceased had left all his assets to his dog Lucky and trusted a friend with the obligation to 'care, feed and annually vaccinate' the dog. The friend claimed the deceased had actually meant to leave his property to him, but the court safely held that the estate (the usual term for the property owned by the deceased) went to the brother of the departed.[7] Only natural persons and charities can inherit and the law still regards animals as property. The proper way of doing it would have been to create a foundation or a trust with the pet as the beneficiary and a person as the trustee. The American Uniform Probate Code even has a provision for this,[8] much to the benefit of the reportedly richest dog in the world. German shepherd Gunther IV regularly eats white truffles, can choose from a wide range of attractive bitches and was able to purchase Madonna's Miami home as a result of the trust that a German countess created to support him and his father Gunther III.[9]

---

6 Cf. Reid, De Waal and Zimmermann 2011, 433.

7 Landgericht Bonn 28 October 2009, 4 T 363/09, openJur 2011, 69514.

8 § 2-907.

9 See www.shortlist.com/shortlists/the-worlds-richest-animals.

The critical question is how much autonomy the testator should have in the disposal of his estate. The law puts three types of limits on the testator's freedom: it restricts the extent to which the testator can dispose of his assets beyond the first generation of heirs, the contents of the will and the extent to which the testator can disinherit his children or spouse.

First, the law restrains the testator's desire to rule from the grave. There is nothing wrong with the testator deciding who should inherit his assets, but it is quite a different thing if he could also rule that the estate will remain with the beneficiary forever or decide that his great-great-great grandchildren will inherit, with all intervening generations only acting as 'provisional heirs' or trustees. If assets are in this way controlled by the 'dead hand', it would not only greatly upset the free marketability of goods but would also restrict social mobility. The rich will stay rich and, much worse, the poor will stay poor. The 1804 French Civil Code therefore prohibited subsequent succession entirely. Today's laws allow for some more, but certainly not unlimited, post-mortem control.[10] German and Dutch law, for example, limit it to a period of maximum 30 years.[11] The common law's way of preventing property from being tied up for too long is the 'rule against perpetuities', which limits the rule by the dead hand in most cases to 125 years (in England) or to 90 years (in most US states).

Public policy and good morals provide a second limit on people's freedom to distribute their assets as they please. What if the testamentary condition holds that only male descendants will inherit, or that the beneficiary must first divorce her husband before obtaining anything? The law has no difficulty in declaring contracts invalid if discriminating on basis of sex, race and religion. But should wills – the expression of private autonomy par excellence – not be treated differently? This is what the English court found in a case in which the beneficiary forfeited all rights under the will by becoming a Roman Catholic. The will was perfectly valid.[12] However, much depends on the goal that the testator wishes to pursue. The motive of the testator in this case was merely to keep up the Protestant tradition in his family and not so much to discriminate against Catholics for being Catholic. This also explains why German courts are happy to accept that nobility can

---

10 Friedman 2009, 4; Dutta 2012, 1631.

11 Art. 4:140 (1) Dutch Civil Code; § 2109 BGB.

12 *Blathwayt v Baron Cawley* [1976] AC 397 (HL).

have a good reason to disinherit male descendants not living up to the family tradition of asking their father's consent before marrying the partner of their choice.[13] And when the receipt of an inheritance by the grandchildren was made dependent on whether or not the grandchild married a spouse of the Jewish faith, an American court reasoned that the wish to encourage and support Judaism and Jewish culture in the family is a good enough motive.[14]

The third limit on freedom of testation, and in practice the most important one, is formed by forced heirship. Forced heirship means that part of the estate is mandatorily reserved for close family members of the deceased. It can come in different forms. Civil law jurisdictions adopt the so-called compulsory portion or *légitime* that gives children (and in some jurisdictions also the spouse or the parents of the deceased) a minimum share in the estate despite the testator's wish to disinherit them.[15] In Romanistic jurisdictions, such as France, Italy and Spain, the testator simply cannot dispose of the part reserved for family members, while Dutch and German law allow the testator to do so but compensate relatives in the form of a claim in cash against the estate. English law has a similar, yet different, institution known as the 'family provision'. If a will fails to make reasonable provision for a child, spouse or other dependant, the court can vary the distribution of the estate. This comes close to the elective share right accepted in the great majority of US states that do not have a matrimonial regime of community property.[16] It allows the disinherited widow or widower, but not the children, to ask the court for a percentage of the deceased's property.

The clear result of all this is that the freedom to do with property as one pleases during life is restricted after death. This is in any event the case when it comes to a European testator wishing to disinherit his children: unlike his American counterpart he will never be able fully to do so. The traditional idea behind forced heirship is to support remaining family members after the death of the breadwinner. Only solidarity among the generations would provide children with a good start in life. However, in today's world the transfer of wealth to the next generation often takes place long before the death of the parents. If parents help

---

13 Bundesverfassungsgericht 21 February 2000, 1937/97 (*Leiningen*).

14 Illinois Supreme Court *In re Estate of Feinberg*, 919 N.E.2d 888 (Ill. 2009).

15 Kroppenberg 2012, 337; De Waal 2006, 1077, 1085.

16 See Section 5.2.1.

out with paying for education or buy a house for their offspring, there may not be much left of the inheritance.[17] In addition, the dramatic increase in life expectancy from 45 years of age in the mid-nineteenth century to 80 today means that by the time their parents die, children are likely to have their own means of income from paid work, savings and pensions. This puts the role of forced heirship as a means of family maintenance into question. Viewed from this perspective English law has it right when it makes the family provision dependent on the actual needs of the children. Louisiana, the only state in the United States with a compulsory portion after the European model, adopted a similar line of thinking when it decided only to appoint children under the age of 24 as forced heirs.[18]

This does not mean that one cannot imagine situations where the American preference for complete freedom to disinherit children seems morally wrong. A daughter may decide to undertake the daily care for her aging mother and make many sacrifices for this, including giving up a full-time job and spending long nights in her mother's house. If, shortly before she dies, the mother writes a will in which she leaves her estate to her son with whom she has a difficult relationship and who has not visited at all in the last five years our intuition tells us that the will is unfair. However, it is quite a different thing to say the law should prevent the mother from exercising her freedom of testation in this way, as European jurisdictions do. Which view must prevail is in the end not a matter of natural law but of political preferences, as De Tocqueville already acknowledged quite some time ago.[19] In inheritance law issues of distributive justice are never far away.

6.3   Intestate succession

The great majority of people do not make wills. They rely on the default rules of intestate succession to deal with their property upon death. This puts a grave responsibility on the legislator who must decide who will inherit, in what order, and what the standard for division must be. There was a time when the estate left by the deceased went to only one of the children, usually the first-born male. For the inheritance of land this so-called primogeniture still existed until 1925 in England. It was a

---

17 Langbein 1988, 735.

18 Art. 1493 (adopted in 1989) of the Louisiana Civil Code.

19 De Tocqueville 1835, Vol. 1, 48.

safe way to make sure land would not have to be carved up among too many descendants. Male primogeniture is still an important feature of indigenous laws but it does not sit easily with the demands of equality posed by state law. This led the Constitutional Court of South Africa to replace black customary law with the rules of intestate succession in a case where two extra-marital daughters claimed a part of their father's inheritance.[20]

Modern systems of intestate succession accept a broader range of heirs. Potential successors to the estate are not only (blood) relatives but also the widow or widower of the deceased (lawyers speak of the surviving spouse). If the deceased had no spouse or children the property goes to the other closest relatives, who could also be the surviving parents or a long-lost auntie. Although all jurisdictions put children or spouses first in line, they show an astonishing variety in the further pecking order of who inherits. It is in the public interest that at some point the property devolves upon the state, but at what point exactly differs from one jurisdiction to another. German and Scots law are happy with the estate going to relatives as remote as the twelfth degree or even beyond, while English law does not accept anyone beyond aunts and uncles.[21] The aim of such restrictions is to avoid the phenomenon of the 'laughing heir', the relative who is far enough in the family line not to mourn over the deceased but close enough to inherit.

The general shift in the last few decades has been from inheritance by the bloodline family to the family of affection.[22] Not too long ago the widow was regarded a stranger to the family and did not necessarily inherit anything. This has changed.[23] Today's legal systems, except for sharia law, all offer a high degree of protection for the surviving spouse, even though they do so in a variety of ways difficult to separate from the applicable matrimonial property regime. Methods range from obtaining the usufruct of the estate (as in France), a share in the ownership of the estate (as in Germany), the whole estate if worth less than £250,000 and half of the excess (as in English law), or the whole estate with a monetary claim of the children against their surviving parent enforceable upon his or her death or bankruptcy (as in Dutch law). In the United States, the surviving spouse gets a third, half or even the

---

20 *Bhe v The Magistrate, Khayelitsha* 2005 (1) SA 580 (CC).

21 Cf. the limits posed by § 2-103 US Uniform Probate Code.

22 Friedman 2009, 11.

23 Reid, De Waal and Zimmermann 2015, 489 ff.

entire estate.[24] The civil partner is usually put in the same position as the surviving spouse, but this is certainly not true for the cohabitee. In many jurisdictions the children of an unmarried couple without a will receive the entire estate while the grieving partner does not receive a cent. The cohabitee may even get evicted from the family home. This calls for inheritance rules that better reflect the realities of modern family life.

A separate question is how the inheritance of the deceased (which usually consists of not only assets but also liabilities) is transferred to the beneficiary. One could imagine that the heir succeeds to the entire bundle of rights and duties, based on the idea that who gets the benefits must also bear the burdens. This is the model of universal succession. If the beneficiary fears the debts outweigh the assets, he can disclaim the inheritance that was automatically transferred to him upon death (as in France and Germany) or must accept the transfer of the estate before it becomes his (as in Austria and Italy). An entirely different model is followed in the common law world. Here the estate typically does not pass to the beneficiaries but to a personal representative of the deceased who is either named in the will (executor) or appointed by the court (administrator). This intermediary deals with the administration of the deceased person's estate in a so-called probate procedure. He settles the debts and transfers the net result of the succession to the heirs and legatees.[25]

These technical differences should not conceal that the result of both testate and intestate succession is that most wealth is inherited and stays within the family.[26] One need not be a meritocrat to argue this may no longer be the right approach if one wants to address social injustices following from extreme inequality in wealth.

24 Cf. Uniform Probate Code § 2-102.
25 Verbeke and Leleu 2011, 463 ff.
26 Beckert 2008.

7   Epilogue

Albert Camus famously wrote that 'life is the sum of all your choices'. Private lawyers could not agree more. The preceding pages abundantly showed that private law allows individuals to know better than the state or anyone else what suits their needs and interests and to act accordingly. People may decide for themselves to contract, to dispose of their property before or after death, to start a family or to claim compensation for other people's unlawful conduct. No one needs to validate my choice to spend all of my time cycling or reading, to work as a lawyer or as a hairdresser or to remain single or get married.[1] However, human flourishing and the well-lived life of one individual are interconnected to and dependent upon other individuals who want to pursue the same.[2] Only Robinson Crusoe did not have to reckon with others. The role of private law, therefore, is not only to empower individuals to pursue their own vision of a distinctively human life – if need be by holding others accountable to them – but also to limit autonomy for the sake of other individuals or the community. The chapters in this book shed light on how the law balances individual autonomy with these countervailing considerations.

The starting point of the law is that individual autonomy can only be a source of obligations when exercised in a meaningful way. The law does not assume that all people are free and equal, but only attaches legal consequences to self-determination that is real, i.e., stems from the freedom a person actually has to do this or be that.[3] To this end, the lawmaker adopts two distinct strategies.

First, private law provides people with alternative courses of action. Instead of leaving the legal organisation of horizontal relationships to the accidental ingenuity (or lack thereof) of the concerned individuals,

---

1 Cf. Lucy 2009, 59.

2 Cf. Alexander and Peñalver 2009, 135.

3 Sen 2009, 231.

the lawmaker facilitates them with pre-set menus of standardised options. This allows people, at least in theory, to predict the consequences of their actions and plan their lives accordingly.[4] Specific contracts, property rights, marriage, civil partnership, divorce and wills are all examples of such options. It is of great help for parties to know that with their purchase, security right, marriage or divorce a whole range of rights and obligations follow that reflect the lawmaker's ideal rules, including protection against imbalanced bargaining power and inequality. Tort also fits into this picture if conceptualised as a vehicle for victims to take voluntary legal action against those who wronged them.[5] According to this view, the law ensures people's access to the resources they need in order for them to flourish.

Second, the concern of the lawmaker is to make sure individuals can freely exercise their autonomy. But here the role of private law is necessarily limited. In an ideal world, everyone has the opportunity to live his or her life as they wish, but the harsh reality is that social, economic, physical, intellectual and educational disparities often stand in their way. For some people opportunity only comes once in a lifetime, if at all. This suggests that addressing issues such as poverty and social injustice likely require means other than what private law can offer. This is not to concede, however, that private law has no role to play in this arena as there are measures empowering individuals to exercise their autonomy in a more meaningful manner. One popular method is to arm individuals with the information necessary to make a rational choice – even though this may not be as effective as the lawmaker envisages.[6]

Finally, even if individual autonomy is exercised in a way that is sufficiently free, it can come into conflict with other essential values the law also needs to protect. This book provided many illustrations of this balancing act. Concerns of distributive justice and protection of third parties were encountered in particular in the law of property, while contract, family and succession law are to a large extent, though not exclusively, characterised by the wish to protect allegedly weaker parties and vulnerable family members. Tort law is special in that it allows the wronged person to be restored to the position he was in prior to the wrong. The exact way in which autonomy and other societal interests

---

4 Dagan 2015, 19.
5 Goldberg and Zipursky 2010.
6 See Section 2.3.

are balanced is always circumstantial and varies greatly over time and space, though more over the former than the latter.

Almost 2,000 years ago, Ulpian formulated three basic principles of the law: live honestly, do not harm others and render each his own.[7] These precepts may be too vague and imprecise to appeal to most contemporary eyes. The message of this book is that a more informative source of essential values on how people should behave can be found in the myriad of nuanced rules that enable people to live together in harmony while preserving their autonomy and individual values. This is what we call private law.

---

7 Institutes of Justinian, I, 1, 3: 'Iuris praecepta sunt haec: honeste vivere, alterum non laedere, suum cuique tribuere'.

References

Ackerman, Bruce (1977), *Private Property and the Constitution*, New Haven, CT: Yale University Press.

Akerlof, George (1970), 'The Market for Lemons: Quality Uncertainty and the Market Mechanism', 84 *Quarterly Journal of Economics* 488–500.

Akkermans, Bram (2008), *The Principle of Numerus Clausus in European Property Law*, Antwerp: Intersentia.

Alexander, Gregory S. (2009), 'The Social-Obligation Norm in American Property Law', 94 *Cornell Law Review* 745–819.

Alexander, Gregory S., and Eduardo M. Peñalver (2009), 'Properties of Community', 10 *Theoretical Inquiries in Law* 127–160.

Aristotle, *Nicomachean Ethics* (350 BCE), (ed. H. Rackham, Loeb Classical Library 73, Cambridge, MA: Harvard University Press 1926).

Atiyah, Patrick (1997), *The Damages Lottery*, Oxford: Hart Publishing.

Barton, Chris, and Gillian Douglas (1995), *Law and Parenthood*, London: Butterworths.

Beale, Hugh, Bénédicte Fauvarque-Cosson, Jacobien Rutgers, Denis Tallon, and Stefan Vogenauer (2010), *Ius Commune Casebooks for the Common Law of Europe: Contract Law*, 2nd edn, Oxford: Hart Publishing.

Beckert, Jens (2008), *Inherited Wealth*, Princeton, NJ: Princeton University Press.

Ben-Shahar, Omri, and Carl E. Schneider (2011), 'The Failure of Mandated Disclosure', 159 *University of Pennsylvania LR* 647–749.

Ben-Shahar, Omri, and Carl E. Schneider (2014), *More Than You Wanted to Know: The Failure of Mandated Disclosure*, Princeton, NJ: Princeton University Press 2014.

Bentham, Jeremy (1789), *An Introduction to the Principles of Morals and Legislation* (eds J. H. Burns and H. L. A. Hart, Oxford: Clarendon Press 1970).

Blackstone, William (1765–69), *Commentaries on the Laws of England* (ed. Wayne Morrison, London: Routledge 2001).

Bowlby, John (1969), *Attachment and Loss: Vol. I Attachment*, New York, NY: Basic Books.

Burrows, Andrew (ed.) (2016), *A Restatement of the English Law of Contract*, Oxford: Oxford University Press.

Bydlinski, Franz (1996), *System und Prinzipien des Privatrechts*, Wien: Springer.

Cane, Peter (2013), *Atiyah's Accidents, Compensation and the Law*, 8th edn, Cambridge: Cambridge University Press.

Capra, Fritjof, and Ugo Mattei (2015), *The Ecology of Law*, Oakland, CA: Berrett-Koehler.

Coase, Ronald H. (1960), 'The Problem of Social Cost', 3 *Journal of Law and Economics* 1–44.

Cohen, Lloyd R. (2002), 'Marriage: The Long-Term Contract', in Anthony W. Dnes and Robert Rowthorn (eds), *The Law and Economics of Marriage and Divorce*, Cambridge: Cambridge University Press, 10–34.

Dagan, Hanoch (2015), 'The Challenges of Private Law: Towards a Research Agenda for an Autonomy-Based Private Law', available at www.papers.ssrn.com/sol3/papers.cfm?abstract_id=2690014.

De Soto, Hernando (2000), *The Mystery of Capital: Why Capitalism Triumphs in the West and Fails Everywhere Else*, New York, NY: Basic Books.

De Tocqueville, Alexis (1835), *Democracy in America* (ed. Phillips Bradley, New York, NY: Knopf 1945).

De Waal, Marius J. (2006), 'Comparative Succession Law', in Mathias Reimann and Reinhard Zimmermann (eds), *The Oxford Handbook of Comparative Law*, Oxford: Oxford University Press, 1071–98.

Denning, A. (1982), *What Next in the Law*, London: Butterworths.

Dewar, John (2003), 'Families', in Peter Cane and Mark Tushnet (eds), *The Oxford Handbook of Legal Studies*, Oxford: Oxford University Press, 413–34.

Dietz, Thomas (2014), *Global Order Beyond Law*, Oxford: Hart Publishing.

Dnes, Antony W. (2002), 'Cohabitation and Marriage', in Anthony W. Dnes and Robert Rowthorn (eds), *The Law and Economics of Marriage and Divorce*, Cambridge: Cambridge University Press, 118–31.

Duguit, Léon (1920), *Les transformations générales du droit privé depuis le Code Napoléon*, 2nd edn, Paris: F. Alcan.

Dutta, Anatol (2012), 'Succession, Subsequent', in Jürgen Basedow, Klaus J. Hopt, and Reinhard Zimmermann (eds), *The Max Planck Encyclopedia of European Private Law*, Oxford: Oxford University Press, 1631–35.

Dwyer, James (2011), *Moral Status and Human Life: The Case for Children's Superiority*, Cambridge: Cambridge University Press.

Eisenberg, Howard B. (1994), 'A "Modest" Proposal: State Licensing of Parents', 26 *Connecticut Law Review* 1415–52.

Epstein, Richard A. (1973), 'A Theory of Strict Liability', 2 *Journal of Legal Studies* 151–204.

Ertman, Martha M. (2015), 'Marital Contracting in a Post-*Windsor* World', 42 *Florida State University LR* 479–520.

Fineman, Martha A. (1995), *The Neutered Mother, the Sexual Family and Other Twentieth Century Tragedies*, London: Routledge.

Fisher, Helen E. (1982), *The Sex Contract: The Evolution of Human Behavior*, New York, NY: William Morrow.

Fleming, John G. (1988), *The American Tort Process*, Oxford: Oxford University Press.

Flume, Werner (1992), *Allgemeiner Teil des Bürgerlichen Rechts, Band 2: Das Rechtsgeschäft*, 4th edn, Berlin: Springer.

Frantz, Carolyn J., and Hanoch Dagan (2004), 'Properties of Marriage', 104 *Columbia Law Review* 75–133.

Fried, Charles (1981), *Contract as Promise: A Theory of Contractual Obligation*, Cambridge, MA: Harvard University Press.

Friedman, Lawrence M. (2009), *Dead Hands: A Social History of Wills, Trusts, and Inheritance Law*, Stanford, CA: Stanford University Press.

Fuller, Lon L., and William R. Perdue (1936), 'The Reliance Interest in Contract Damages', 46 *Yale Law Journal* 52–96, 373–420.

Gadoua, Susan Pease, and Vicki Larson (2014), *The New 'I Do'*, Berkeley: Seal Press.

Gilmore, Grant (1954), 'The Commercial Doctrine of Good Faith Purchase', 63 *Yale Law Journal* 1057–122.

Glendon, Mary-Ann (1989), *The Transformation of Family Law: State, Law, and Family in the United States and Western Europe*, Chicago, IL: University of Chicago Press.

Goldberg, John C. P., and Benjamin C. Zipursky (2010), 'Torts as Wrongs', 88 *Texas Law Review* 917.

Goode, Roy (1992), 'The Concept of Good Faith in English Law', in *Saggi, Conferenze e Seminari 2*, Rome: Centro di studi e ricerche di diritto comparato e straniero.

Gordley, James (2006), *Foundations of Private Law: Property, Tort, Contract, Unjust Enrichment*, Oxford: Oxford University Press.

Gordon, Wendy J. (2003), 'Intellectual Property', in Peter Cane and Mark Tushnet (eds), *The Oxford Handbook of Legal Studies*, Oxford: Oxford University Press 617–46.

Grotius, Hugo (1625), *De Iure Belli ac Pacis* ('The Rights of War and Peace', ed. Richard Tuck, Indianapolis, IN: Liberty Fund).

Gutmann, Thomas (2013), 'Some Preliminary Remarks on a Liberal Theory of Contract', 76 *Law and Contemporary Problems* 39–55.

Halley, Janet, and Kerry Rittich (2010), 'Critical Directions in Comparative Family Law', 58 *American Journal of Comparative Law* 753–75.

Hardin, Garrett (1968), 'The Tragedy of the Commons', 162 *Science* 1243–48.

Heise, A. (1807), *Grundriss eines Systems des gemeinen Civilrechts*, Heidelberg: Mohr und Zimmer.

Heller, Michael A. (1998), 'The Tragedy of the Anticommons', 111 *Harvard Law Review* 625.

Heller, Michael A. (2003), 'Property', in Peter Cane and Mark Tushnet (eds), *The Oxford Handbook of Legal Studies*, Oxford: Oxford University Press, 62–79.

Helsen, Frederic (2015), 'Security in Movables Revisited: Belgium's Rethinking of the Article 9 UCC System', *European Review of Private Law* 959–1026.

Herring, Jonathan (2013), *Caring and the Law*, Oxford: Hart Publishing.

Herring, Jonathan (2014), *Family law: A Very Short Introduction*, Oxford: Oxford University Press.

Herring, Jonathan, Rebecca Probert, and Stephen Gilmore (2015), *Great Debates in Family Law*, 2nd edn, London: Palgrave.

Hohfeld, Wesley (1946), *Fundamental Legal Conceptions as Applied in Judicial Reasoning*, New Haven, CT: Yale University Press.

Holmes, Oliver Wendell (1881), *The Common Law* (ed. Mark de Wolfe Howe, Cambridge, MA: Harvard University Press 1963).

Horwitz, Morton (1977), *The Transformation of American Law 1780–1860*, Cambridge, MA: Harvard University Press.

Jansen, Nils (2010), *The Making of Legal Authority*, Oxford: Oxford University Press.

Jensen, Michael C. (1998), *Foundations of Organizational Strategy*, Cambridge, MA: Harvard University Press.

Kaplow, Louis, and Steven Shavell (2002), *Fairness versus Welfare*, Cambridge, MA: Harvard University Press.

Kennedy, Duncan (2010), 'Savigny's Family/Patrimony Distinction and its Place in the Global Genealogy of Classical Legal Thought', 58 *American Journal of Comparative Law* 811–41.

Kessler, Friedrich (1943), 'Contracts of Adhesion: Some Thoughts About Freedom of Contract', 43 *Columbia Law Review* 629–42.

Keynes, John Maynard (1936), *The General Theory of Employment, Interest and Money*, London: Macmillan.

Kornhauser, Lewis, and Robert Mnookin (1979), 'Bargaining in the Shadow of the Law: The Case of Divorce', 88 *Yale Law Journal* 954–97.

Krause, Harry D. (2006), 'Comparative Family Law', in Mathias Reimann and Reinhard Zimmermann (eds), *The Oxford Handbook of Comparative Law*, Oxford: Oxford University Press, 1100–29.

Kronman, Anthony T. (1980), 'Contract Law and Distributive Justice' 89 *Yale Law Journal* 472–511.

Kroppenberg, Inge (2012), 'Compulsory Portion', in Jürgen Basedow et al. (eds), *The Max Planck Encyclopedia of European Private Law*, Oxford: Oxford University Press, 337–41.

Langbein, John H. (1988), 'The Twentieth-Century Revolution in Family Wealth Transmission', 86 *Michigan Law Review* 722–51.

Lawson, F. H., and Bernard Rudden (2002), *The Law of Property*, 3rd edn, Oxford: Oxford University Press.

Llewellyn, Karl (1939), 'Our Case-Law of Contract Offer and Acceptance II', 48 *Yale Law Journal* 779–818.

Locke, John (1689), *Two Treatises of Government* (ed. P. Laslett, Cambridge: Cambridge University Press 1960).

Lucy, William (2009), 'What's Private about Private Law?', in Andrew Robertson and Hang Wu Tang (eds), *The Goals of Private Law*, Oxford: Hart Publishing, 47–75.

Macaulay, Stewart (1963), 'Non-Contractual Relations in Business: A Preliminary Study', 28 *American Sociological Review* 55–67.

Macneil, Ian R. (1978), 'Contracts: Adjustment of Long-Term Economic Relations under Classical, Neoclassical and Relational Contract Law', 72 *Northwestern University Law Review* 854–902.

Maine, Henry Sumner (1861), *Ancient Law*, London: John Murray.

Markovits, Daniel (2014), 'Good Faith as Contract's Core Value', in Gregory Klass, George Letsas, and Prince Saprai (eds), *Philosophical Foundations of Contract Law*, Oxford: Oxford University Press, 272–92.

Mattei, Ugo (2000), *Basic Principles of Property Law: A Comparative Legal and Economic Introduction*, Westport, CT: Greenwood Press.

Montesquieu (1748), *De l'Esprit des Lois* ('The Spirit of the Laws', ed. Anne M. Cohler, Basia C. Miller, and Harold S. Stone, Cambridge: Cambridge University Press 1989).

Munzer, Stephen R (1990), *A Theory of Property*, Cambridge: Cambridge University Press.

Nelson, Erin (2013), *Law, Policy and Reproductive Autonomy*, Oxford: Hart Publishing.

Nozick, Robert (1974), *Anarchy, State and Utopia*, New York, NY: Basic Books.

Overall, Christine (2012), *Why Have Children? The Ethical Debate*, Cambridge, MA: MIT Press.

Piketty, Thomas (2014), *Capital in the Twenty-First Century*, Cambridge, MA: Harvard University Press.

Plato (380 BCE), *Republic* (Vol. 1, ed. Chris Emlyn-Jones and William Preddy, Loeb Classical Library 237, Cambridge, MA: Harvard University Press 2013).

Portalis (1803), 'Exposé des motifs' (ed. M. Locré, *Législation Civile, Commerciale et Criminelle, tome 4*, Bruxelles: H. Tarlier 1836).

Posner, Eric A. (2000), *Law and Social Norms*, Cambridge, MA: Harvard University Press.

Posner, Richard A. (1992), *Sex and Reason*, Cambridge, MA: Harvard University Press.

Posner, Richard A. (2014), *Economic Analysis of Law*, 9th edn, New York, NY: Wolters Kluwer.

Probert, Rebecca (2012), *The Changing Legal Regulation of Cohabitation*, Cambridge: Cambridge University Press.

Prosser, William (1984), *Handbook of the Law of Torts*, 5th edn, St Paul, MN: West.

Rawls, John (1971), *A Theory of Justice* (revised edn, Cambridge, MA: Harvard University Press 1999).

Rawls, John (2001), *Justice as Fairness: A Restatement*, Cambridge, MA: Harvard University Press.

Reich, Charles (1964), 'The New Property: Government Largess, Wealth and Property', 73 *Yale Law Journal* 733–87.

Reid, Kenneth G. C., Marius J. de Waal, and Reinhard Zimmermann (eds) (2011), *Comparative Succession Law*, Vol. 1, Oxford: Oxford University Press.

Reid, Kenneth G. C., Marius J. de Waal, and Reinhard Zimmermann (eds) (2015), *Comparative Succession Law*, Vol. 2, Oxford: Oxford University Press.

Rousseau, Jean-Jacques (1755), *Discours sur l'origine et les fondements de l'inégalité parmi les hommes* ('Discourse on the Origin of Inequality', ed. Donald A. Cress, Indianapolis, IN: Hackett 1992).

Rudden, Bernard (1987), 'Economic Theory v. Property Law: The Numerus Clausus Problem', in John Eekelaar and John Bell (eds), *Oxford Essays on Jurisprudence*, 3rd edn, Oxford: Oxford University Press, 239–63.

Scherpe, Jens M. (2012), 'Marital Agreements', in Jürgen Basedow et al. (eds), *The Max Planck Encyclopedia of European Private Law*, Oxford: Oxford University Press, 1134–8.

Schneider, Carl E. (1992), 'The Channelling Function in Family Law', 20 *Hofstra Law Review* 495–532.

Sen, Amartya (2009), *The Idea of Justice*, Cambridge, MA: Belknap Press.

Singer, Peter (1981), *The Expanding Circle: Ethics, Evolution, and Moral Progress*, Princeton, NJ: Princeton University Press.

Smart, Carol, and Bren Neale (1999), *Family fragments?*, Cambridge: Polity Press.

Smith, Adam (1776), *An Inquiry into the Nature and Causes of the Wealth of Nations* (ed. Kathryn Sutherland, Oxford: Oxford University Press 1993).

Smith, Stephen A. (2011), 'The Normativity of Private Law', 31 *Oxford Journal of Legal Studies* 215–42.

Smits, Jan (2014), *Contract Law: A Comparative Introduction*, Cheltenham, UK and Northampton, MA, USA: Edward Elgar Publishing.

Trebilcock, Michael J. (1993), *The Limits of Freedom of Contract*, Cambridge, MA: Harvard University Press.

Van Caenegem, R. C. (1992), *Judges, Legislators and Professors*, Cambridge: Cambridge University Press.

Van Dam, Cees (2013), *European Tort Law*, 2nd edn, Oxford: Oxford University Press.

Van Erp, Sjef, and Bram Akkermans (2012), *Ius Commune Casebooks for the Common Law of Europe: Property Law*, Oxford: Hart Publishing.

Verbeke, Alain (2001), 'Naar een billijk relatievermogensrecht', 38 *Tijdschrift voor Privaatrecht* 373–402.

Verbeke, Alain, and Yves-Henri Leleu (2011), 'Harmonization of the Law of Succession in Europe', in Arthur S. Hartkamp, Martijn W. Hesselink, Ewoud Hondius, Chantal Mak, and Edgar du Perron (eds), *Towards a European Civil Code*, 4th edn, Alphen aan den Rijn: Kluwer Law International, 459–79.

Von Savigny, F. C. (1840–49), *System des heutigen römischen Rechts* ('System of the Modern Roman Law', ed. William Holloway, Westport, CT: Hyperion Press 1979).

Wagner, Gerhard (2006), 'Comparative Tort Law', in Mathias Reimann and Reinhard Zimmermann (eds), *The Oxford Handbook of Comparative Law*, Oxford: Oxford University Press, 1003–41.

Waldron, Jeremy (1988), *The Right to Private Property*, New York, NY: Oxford University Press.

Warren, Samuel, and Louis Brandeis (1890), 'The Right to Privacy', 4 *Harvard Law Review* 193–220.

Weber, Max (1922), *Wirtschaft und Gesellschaft* ('Economy and Society', eds Günther Roth and Claus Wittich, Berkeley, CA: University of California Press 1978).

Weinrib, Ernest J. (1995), *The Idea of Private Law*, Cambridge, MA: Harvard University Press.

Weir, Tony (2006), *An Introduction to Tort Law*, 2nd edn, Oxford: Oxford University Press.

World Bank (2016), *Doing Business 2016: Measuring Regulatory Quality and Efficiency*, 13th edn, Washington, DC.

Zimmermann, Reinhard (1990), *The Law of Obligations: Roman Foundations of the Civilian Tradition*, Cape Town: Juta.

Index

Titles in the **Elgar Advanced Introductions** series include: